UNDERSTANDING
SPORT PSYCHOLOGY

ACTIVITIES FOR PUTTING IT ALL TOGETHER

Melanie Gregg
The University of Winnipeg

Barbi Law
Nipissing University

Jenny O
California State University, East Bay

Kim Davies

Kendall Hunt
publishing company

Cover image courtesy of Daniel Gregg

Kendall Hunt
publishing company

www.kendallhunt.com

Send all inquiries to:
4050 Westmark Drive
Dubuque, IA 52004-1840

Printed in the United States of America
10 9 8 7 6 5 4 3 2 1

CONTENTS

Melanie Gregg is an associate professor in the Faculty of Kinesiology and Applied Health at the University of Winnipeg where she teaches sport and exercise psychology. Dr. Gregg has a bachelor's of physical education and a master's of science in physical education (specializing in sport psychology) both from the University of Manitoba. She completed her PhD in the School of Kinesiology at the University of Western Ontario. Since that time she has completed a coaching internship for the sport of track and field through the Coaching Association of Canada. Dr. Gregg's research interests are predominantly in examining the role of mental imagery in performance enhancement, particularly the motivational function of imagery. Additionally she has interests in studying coaching behaviours and the use of psychological skills by athletes with intellectual disability. Dr. Gregg has consulted with athletes from a variety of team and individual sports. As a former athlete in the heptathlon Dr. Gregg gives back to the track and field community by coaching high school, provincial- and national-level athletes. She continues to be active and regularly plays organized volleyball and touch football. She is also an outdoor enthusiast and takes every opportunity to hike, canoe, and ski.

Lead author: Chapters 1, 5, 7, and 11.

Barbi Law is an assistant professor of sport and exercise psychology in the School of Physical and Health Education at Nipissing University in North Bay, ON. Dr. Law completed her honors bachelor's degree in kinesiology at McMaster University, her master's in motor learning at the University of Ottawa, and her PhD in sport and exercise psychology at the University of Western Ontario. Her research program seeks to understand how psychological skills, such as imagery and modeling, can be used to enhance both physical and psychological performance in a variety of movement environments. Specifically, Dr. Law is interested in how modeling interventions can be best designed to enhance individuals' self-regulation, skill learning, and performance in sport, exercise, and injury rehabilitation settings. She also examines psychological skill use among coaches. Recently, her research has expanded to explore how imagery can be used to enhance students' physical education experiences. Dr. Law is a former figure skater, with sport experience as an instructor and coach as well. Currently, she provides sport psychology consulting services to both coaches and athletes. She has consulted with both team and individual sport groups, from the grassroots to the national level.

Lead author: Chapters 3, 8, and 12.

Jenny O is an assistant professor in kinesiology at California State University, East Bay. Dr. O completed her honors degree in sport and physical education at Laurentian University, her master's degree in sport psychology at the University of Windsor, and her PhD in sport and exercise psychology at the University of Western Ontario. Dr. O's main interest is in examining and understanding ways in which athletes can use psychological skills and cognitive processes to maximize optimal performance in high-pressure environments. She focuses her research on the manipulation of mental images by athletes, and, in particular, on the functional advantages of voluntary image speed manipulation. She also examines psychological skills transfer: the transfer of psychological skills learned in one performance context to another. Dr. O is an expert on psychological skills use in sport, and actively provides sport psychology consulting services to North American sport teams as well as to individual athletes. She has worked with numerous team and individual sport populations and has also provided performance psychology services to individuals and groups outside of sport, in performance domains such as business, politics, military, the performing arts, and social networking. Dr. O is a former athlete and has competed extensively in women's baseball. She also has extensive baseball and softball coaching and player development experience from the grassroots through the national level.

Lead author: Chapters 2, 6, and 10.

Kim Davies is a performance consultant specializing in helping athletes achieve and sustain optimal performance. Dr. Davies completed her honors degree in psychology at University of Toronto, her master's degree in sport psychology at McGill University, and her PhD in sport and exercise psychology at the University of Western Ontario. Over the past ten years, Dr. Davies has consulted with elite-level athletes from across Canada. Clients have included individual athletes and teams competing in the Olympics and Canada Games, as well as within a variety of professional, intercollegiate, and amateur leagues. Dr. Davies is a registered professional member with the Canadian Sport Psychology Association (CSPA). Dr. Davies has also published extensive research in the areas of group dynamics, peak performance, and aggression in sport. Dr. Davies is a former elite-level hockey and ringette player and has experience coaching provincial teams in both sports.

Lead author: Chapters 4 and 9.

Contributor

Daniel Gregg is an artist specializing in acrylic paintings. His subject matter is diverse and he has contributed the cover art as well as a drawing in Chapter 2 to this book.

HOW TO USE *UNDERSTANDING SPORT PSYCHOLOGY: ACTIVITIES FOR PUTTING IT ALL TOGETHER!*

Purpose of the Book

This book is a supplement to your course textbook. Each chapter focuses on a topic included in many of the popular textbooks used in introductory sport and exercise psychology courses. Your instructor may assign specific chapters of this supplement for you to complete at specific points in the course, or you can work through the chapters on your own as you cover related material in your course. The chapters are to help you test your knowledge of each topic and identify areas where you may have questions or need to review the material in greater depth.

Each chapter illustrates concepts and theories through the experiences of specific athlete scenarios, bringing sport psychology to life, and demonstrating how to apply the concepts in real life. Practical and self-reflective activities challenge you to apply the concepts not only to the world around you, but to your own life as well. Though the athlete scenarios, practical, and self-reflective activities are evidence-based, this supplement is not heavy on references and research language. Rather, each chapter refers you to suggested readings and texts that elaborate on the concepts in greater detail. As this is a supplement, the assumption is that you are familiar with the concepts in each chapter and are using the activities to test the limits of your knowledge and ability to apply the concepts.

Completing the activities in the book will help you to clarify sport psychology concepts and to apply them to sport and exercise specific scenarios. You may also want to think about whether the concepts can be applied to other scenarios in your life. This book may also be of interest to athletes, coaches, parents, those seeking to develop an applied practice (e.g., psychologists who may not have experience working with athletes, kinesiology graduate students), and individuals who have an interest in applying sport psychology concepts to other areas of their life (e.g., workplace, leisure pursuits, academics, interpersonal relationships).

Each chapter is written in a conversational style—think of it as a conversation between a student and an instructor, sport psychology consultant, or teaching assistant. The text is meant to get you thinking about the topics, and help you make connections between concepts, as well as between concepts and everyday experiences. Each chapter is broken down into several sections. Below is a description of each.

Athlete Scenarios

Each chapter begins with an athlete scenario. To help you see the connections between topics and get to know the athletes in more depth, the same athletes are used throughout this book. While each of the athlete profiles below represents a fictional athlete, each is based on typical scenarios encountered by athletes, and is drawn from research and our practical experiences as athletes, coaches, and sport psychology consultants. As sport psychology applies to athletes of all ages and ability levels, we have attempted to create profiles that represent a range of athletes. Read through the profiles below to become acquainted with each of the athlete profiles. The chapters will introduce you to these athletes in more depth.

Joe: Professional Athlete

Meet Joe, a professional hockey player in the National Hockey League (NHL). Joe grew up on a reserve in northern Manitoba and played hockey for his high school. He was the star right wing for his university team and was drafted to play in the NHL. So far Joe has had a long and successful career in the NHL but is finding it challenging to meet the physical and psychological demands of continuing to play at the elite level. As a professional athlete Joe is required to perform on the ice as well as off; he has an image to project to the media and his fans. As he is getting older Joe is looking toward retiring from hockey and planning his future.

Laura: National Team Athlete

Laura plays wheelchair basketball with the national team. The team is working toward the next Paralympic competition. This is an important competition for a couple of reasons: the team is the defending champion and the funding for the national team is partly based on their results at this competition. Because the team is not centralized (in one location, training together year-round) they have several training camps each year that the team members must travel to and participate in. Laura and her team must face these challenges, as well as challenges related to travel logistics, getting time off of work for training camps and competitions, and working together as a team.

Ashley: High School Athlete

Ashley, a grade 11 student, plays on several teams at her high school: volleyball, basketball, badminton, curling, and soccer. She's had quite a lot of success at all of these sports at the high school level but knows that she needs to start focusing on one or two sports in order to compete at the Canada Games and have coaches notice her for their university programs. Ashley has spent some time talking to her school guidance counsellor, parents, and coaches, for their advice on how to decide what sport she should focus on.

Owen: Youth Sport Athlete

Owen is 8 years old and plays soccer in the summer and hockey in the winter. Owen knows his mom and dad try hard to get him to practices and to games, but sometimes it's tough as they live in a rural area. He would love to play softball but is worried about asking his parents because it will cost even more money and require more driving by his parents. Owen is enjoying soccer and hockey but would like to try a new sport.

Kayla: Varsity Athlete

Kayla is a student-athlete who is a member of the swim team at a large university in Ontario. Kayla is busy in the pool and doing dry land training for about 20 hours per week. On top of that she is a full-time kinesiology student and has a part-time job for 5 hours per week at a local coffee shop. Finding time to spend with family and friends is sometimes difficult, but Kayla has decided sport and school are her priorities for now.

Eric: Recreational Athlete

Eric is 36 years old, works at a desk job for the federal government, is married to Melissa, and has two young children. Recently Eric has noticed he lacks the energy to play with his kids. He used to play sports in high school but since then has not been very active. He's also concerned about his health; last year his dad was diagnosed with diabetes. Eric is exploring options to be more active for both health and social benefits. Activities he has considered joining are recreational coed volleyball (he and Melissa could play together), a neighbourhood early morning bootcamp, and the badminton program at the nearby racquet club.

Key Concepts and Theories

At the beginning of each chapter is a list of key concepts and theories that you should be familiar with before completing the activities within the chapter. These are concepts that are likely covered within your course and that are important for being able to complete the activities within the supplement chapter. If you are unfamiliar with a concept, go back and review your textbook chapter on that topic, or check with your instructor about which concepts are important to understand in your course.

Deep Thoughts

Throughout the chapter, the text will be broken up with Deep Thoughts. These represent opportunities for you to stop and reflect on the concepts presented up to that point in the chapter. The Deep Thoughts provide you with reflective activities that you can do in class, on your own, or with a study buddy.

Try It Out!

At the end of each chapter is a series of activities designed to give you an opportunity to try out various concepts presented within the chapter. Each activity focuses on a specific concept or group of concepts. Think of these as checkpoints within the chapter to make sure you understand each of the concepts on their own. Within the text you are prompted to do specific activities at specific checkpoints.

Putting it All Together

The final activity within each chapter focuses on your ability to make connections between concepts and apply those concepts to a real-world example. This might be applying the concepts to one of the athlete scenarios or to your own life. Think of these as your way of testing your knowledge of each topic as it fits into the "big picture" of sport and exercise performance.

Suggested Readings

At the end of each chapter is a list of suggested readings. These include references cited within the chapter, as well as reference articles and books that will help you to learn more about each topic. The suggested readings also refer to popular introductory sport and exercise texts that cover that topic.

Starting Your Journey

Now that you have a clear idea of how each chapter is organized, we encourage you to explore the book. Based on your course syllabus, identify which chapters apply to each topic your instructor will cover and then work your way through the activities in the supplement as you progress through the course. We hope that the athlete scenarios and activities will help you to increase your knowledge and understanding of sport psychology, but most importantly, we hope that this book will help you to see how you can apply these concepts to your own life.

Chapter 1

Welcome to Sport and Exercise Psychology

Key Concepts and Theories

- Definitions of sport and exercise psychology
- Roles of sport and exercise psychologists
- Licensing and certification
- Psychological (mental) skills

Performing to Potential

Joe: "Hey coach."
Coach: "Hi Joe, how are you?"
J: "I'm fine."
C: "Are you sure? You seem a bit sluggish lately."
J: "Yeah."
C: "Is something bothering you?"
J: "Well, I feel as though I'm putting in a lot of work during training but I'm just not performing as well as I'd like in our preseason games."
C: "Are you feeling alright physically? Any injuries?"
J: "I feel great, even my testing in weight training is going well."
C: "Hmmm … maybe it's time to see Dr. Smith, the mental training consultant for our team. Sport psychology helps me, as a coach, to be more confident, focused, and motivated. It also helps a lot of your teammates perform to their potential. Maybe it can help you too."
J: "I don't know. I'm not sure about sitting on a couch and talking to a shrink."
C: "It's not really like that Joe. The mental trainer will meet you in his office or at the rink, wherever you feel comfortable. He's focused on helping you perform better in hockey, not to solve all of your problems in life. I think you should give it a shot. What do you have to lose?"
J: "Alright, I'll give it a try. Thanks coach."

In the opening scene we see that Joe, a professional athlete, is struggling with underperforming in competition. After ruling out the potential of injury or other physical problems the coach suggests seeing a mental training consultant. Athletes seek out mental trainers or sport psychologists for many reasons, and most often it is to gain an edge when performing rather than to treat a specific problem.

Defining Sport and Exercise Psychology

Human behaviour in sport and exercise environments is the central tenet of sport and exercise psychology. Conversely, the influence of participation in sport and exercise activities on psychological well-being is also a reflection of sport and exercise psychology. To illustrate these points, Joe's underperformance in a competitive environment is a reflection of his behaviour in the sport setting. In turn, this underperformance is causing Joe to feel downhearted and to lose confidence in his abilities.

Where Did Sport and Exercise Psychology Come From?

Sport psychology has been around longer than most people realize. In 1898 Norman Triplett, an American psychologist, was interested in how the presence of others affected the performance of cyclists.

Deep Thought

Why would the athletes perform best in pairs? A phenomenon called *social loafing* is one explanation. How do you perform on your own versus with a friend?

What about compared to when you are in a large group?

© Ljupco Smokovski, 2012. Used under license from Shutterstock, Inc.

Triplett compared cyclists riding alone, in pairs, and in groups. He found the cyclists performed best in pairs. Triplett's study was the first recorded study to involve the psychology of athletes.

Since Triplett's initial study in sport many academic journals have been published that are specifically oriented to sport and exercise psychology (see the Resource list at the end of this chapter). The development of professional organizations, each with several hundred members, help sport psychologists continue their professional development through regular professional meetings, workshops, publishing journals, and as a venue to present current research (see the Resource list at the end of this chapter for the websites of these organizations). The field of sport psychology has certainly grown since Triplett's time, and more people are seeing the benefits of applying sport psychology to their performance on and off the field.

A Day in the Life of Sport and Exercise Psychologists

Sport and exercise psychologists are trained in the psychological aspects of sport, physical activity, and exercise. Licensed psychologists who have a focus on sport are licensed by their province of residence to practice psychology and may have clients outside of sport. Licensed psychologists not only help athletes to improve performance, but they are also able to assist with clinical issues such as disordered eating, depression, and substance abuse. Licensed psychologists have a professional degree in psychology from a recognized university, have completed appropriate training including supervised internships, and have been licensed through provincial legislation to practice psychology.

Sport psychology consultants who are not licensed have generally been trained through kinesiology departments with a minimum of a master's degree. Individuals who are in private practice are not licensed to use the title *psychologist*, so often they will be referred to as mental training consultants, mental trainers, and the like. The role of these consultants, generally, is to educate coaches and athletes and help athletes develop psychological skills (such as coping under pressure, time management, communication, etc.). Unlicensed consultants are not qualified to help athletes with clinical issues; however, if these issues are evident, then the consultant is responsible for referring the athlete to an appropriate resource. Dr. Smith, the sport psychology consultant mentioned in the vignette at the beginning of this chapter, has a PhD in kinesiology and is not a licensed psychologist. Because of his training Dr. Smith must stay within his scope of practice, or in other words, within the boundaries of his training (see the list of Resources near the end of this chapter for where to access ethical guidelines for sport psychology consultants).

Aside from consulting with athletes, teams, and coaches, many sport psychologists work in academic settings where their roles include teaching university students and conducting research. Usually consultants who work at a university have doctorate degrees. In recent years researchers and consultants have begun to focus more on exercise and physical activity. This shift is timely given the declining rates of activity of Canadians and, in particular, young Canadians. The benefits of a physically active lifestyle to both psychological and physical health have been well documented. It is the role of researchers and consultants of exercise psychology to find ways to get Canadians to initiate and maintain physical activity. Throughout this book the focus is on sport psychology rather than on exercise psychology, though many of the concepts from sport are also useful in exercise contexts. For more on exercise and physical activity see Chapter 12. Reflect on what factors have influenced your own participation in sport and exercise by completing Try It Out! Activity 1 on page 7.

Dr. Smith: "Hi, you must be Joe. Come on in. Coach said you would be stopping by. How are you?"

Joe: "Hello Dr. Smith. I'm alright, how are you?"

S: "I'm great. Please call me Mike."

J: "Okay, thanks."

S: "I just want to clarify a few things before we start, Joe. I am not a licensed psychologist, so I don't deal with any clinical issues. My role is to help athletes reach their peak performance by identifying some psychological strategies that may help them. There may be some techniques you find very helpful, whereas others you may not use often or you don't like. That's okay. Each athlete is different, and some of these techniques work better for some than for others. Just because you've come to see me doesn't mean you have a problem, it just means there is some room for improvement and it's possible that working on your psychological skills will help you to improve your hockey performance. It's important to remember that there are *no quick fixes* and that psychological skills must be practiced, just like physical skills, in order to see improvements and to use the skills effectively. Whatever we talk about in our sessions will be confidential and I won't discuss what you say with anyone else, unless you request me to."

J: "Okay, that all sounds reasonable. How many sessions will we have?"

S: "That varies with each individual athlete. Some athletes like to meet regularly, such as a couple of times a week, for a brief amount of time each. Others only meet with me three or four times and then have occasional follow-up sessions later on. We'll have to see how everything progresses. Any other questions?"

J: "Not that I can think of right now."

S: "Alright, if any come to mind later, just ask. Here's my card with my phone numbers and e-mail address on it so you can easily reach me if you need anything."

J: "Great, thanks."

S: "I like to start with a questionnaire that assesses how you currently use psychological skills. I find this a useful starting point to give me a better understanding of where you're coming from, and it's usually a good way to start a discussion. It will take about fifteen minutes to complete. Do you want to do it now?"

J: "Sure, let's get started."

Vignette 2 illustrates what may happen during the first meeting of a sport psychology consultant and an athlete. During this first meeting the consultant and athlete will get a feel for whether there is a compatible match and if they will be able to work together successfully. In this session the consultant will address some of the housekeeping issues that may include the number of sessions, expectations of the athlete, the consultant's role, fees, and the consultant's theoretical perspective.

Many athletes seek sport psychology support when they, or their coach, believe the athlete is underperforming in competition compared to training, performs better in less-important competitions than in more important ones, wants to reach the next level of competition, lacks motivation or focus during training, or

Deep Thought

What are some qualities that would make an effective consultant (e.g., knowledgeable)? What are some qualities that would make an ineffective consultant (e.g., tries to take on the role of coach)?

is frustrated with his or her environment or performance. It is evident from vignette 1 that Joe feels he is underperforming in competition compared to training and is frustrated with his performance. There are many methods of assessing an athlete's current use of psychological skills: one-on-one interviews, psychological skills inventories (see the Resources section of this chapter for a list of inventories that assess multiple psychological skills), or observation. Some of these inventories assess a variety of psychological skills, such as the Ottawa Mental Skills Assessment tool, whereas others provide a comprehensive evaluation of a single psychological skill: the Movement Imagery Questionnaire specifically assesses an athlete's imagery ability for example. Dr. Smith is using a combination of psychological skills inventory and one-on-one interview to determine Joe's current use of psychological skills. Following these assessments Dr. Smith will be able to plan future sessions to help Joe. Complete Try It Out! Activity 2 on page 7 to assess your own mental skills.

Summary: Putting It All Together

Sport and exercise psychology are not just for *problem athletes*; all athletes can benefit from improving their psychological skills. Sport psychology consultants work together with athletes and coaches to assess an athlete's needs and to devise strategies to help the athlete reach their peak performance. Qualified sport psychology consultants will engage in evidence-based practice: this means they use theory and research from reliable sources to guide their practice. By using this book in conjunction with a basic introductory sport psychology textbook students will gain a more practical understanding of how sport psychology works. Coaches, parents, consultants, and athletes can also learn more about sport psychology by engaging in the Putting It All Together activity on page 8.

Resources

Sport and Exercise Psychology Journals

Athletic Insight: The Online Journal of Sport Psychology
European Journal of Sport Science
International Journal of Sport and Exercise Psychology
International Journal of Sport Psychology
International Review of Sport and Exercise Psychology
Journal of Applied Sport Psychology
Journal of Clinical Sport Psychology
Journal of Imagery Research in Sport and Physical Activity
Journal of Sport and Exercise Psychology
Journal of Sport and Exercise Sciences
Perceptual and Motor Skills
Psychology of Sport and Exercise
Research Quarterly for Exercise and Sport
The Sport Psychologist

Professional Organizations and Websites

Association for Applied Sport Psychology http://appliedsportpsych.org/
The British Association of Sport and Exercise Sciences http://www.bases.org.uk/
Canadian Psychological Association http://www.cpa.ca/
Canadian Society for Psychomotor Learning and Sport Psychology http://www.scapps.org/
Canadian Sport Psychology Association http://www.en.cspa-acps.ca/
European Federation of Sport Psychology http://www.fepsac.com/
International Society of Sport Psychology http://www.issponline.org/
North American Society for the Psychology of Sport and Physical Activity http://www.naspspa.org/
The Psychological Association of Manitoba http://www.cpmb.ca/
Note: All of these websites include valuable resources for the ethical conduct of sport psychology consultants.

Physical Activity Participation Rates

Canadian Fitness and Lifestyle Research Institute http://www.cflri.ca/eng/levels/index.php

Psychological Skills Inventories

Athletic Coping Skills Inventory-28 (ACSI-28; Smith & Smoll, 1995)
Ottawa Mental Skills Assessment Tool (OMSAT-3; Durand-Bush, Salmela, & Green, 2001)
Psychological Skills Inventory for Sports (PSIS and PSIS R-5; Mahoney, Gabriel, & Perkins, 1987; Mahoney, 1989)
Test of Performance Strategies (TOPS; Thomas, Murphy, & Hardy, 1999)

Try It Out!

Activity 1: Factors Related to Participation

Take some time to reflect on your past experiences with sport and physical activity. Describe how those past experiences influence your present participation. Some things to think about might be who influenced your participation, the activity level of your family, the facilities available in the community you grew up in, both positive and negative experiences with participation, and more.

Activity 2: Assessing Mental Skills

Your instructor will provide a psychological skills inventory. Many are available online (see the Resources list for suggestions). Think about the primary sport you participate in (as athlete, coach, official, etc.) and answer the psychological skills inventory in relation to your participation. Report your results below and indicate what areas need improvement. Brainstorm how this improvement in psychological skills may lead to advances in sport performance. (*Note:* It is sometimes helpful for the athlete to complete an inventory and the coach to complete the same one on his or her perspective of the athlete and then to compare the results. Are there discrepancies between the results?)

Putting It All Together

Read the following story and use the Canadian Psychological Association's (CPA; http://www.cpa.ca/) ethical code to identify what principles apply to the story. Illustrate why the principles apply, and describe the most ethical way for Dr. Smith to proceed.

Dr. Smith has been working as a consultant with a professional hockey team for the past five years. For the most part, Dr. Smith's role involves meeting with the team and educating the players about various psychological skills, such as self-talk, time management, and building team cohesion. Occasionally an athlete will request, or the coach will recommend, an individual meeting. At the start of each season Dr. Smith explains his role and expectations to the athletes and reminds the athletes that he is not a licensed psychologist. Last week the coach suggested Joe meet with Dr. Smith on an individual basis. The coach tells Dr. Smith that Joe has not been performing up to his potential. The coach is also concerned about Joe's future with the team if he is not able to perform. To make sure his athlete will perform better and remain on the team the coach requests regular progress reports from Dr. Smith.

Suggested Readings and References

Cox, R. H. (2007). *Sport psychology: Concepts and applications*, 6th ed. New York: McGraw-Hill.

Crocker, P. R. E. (2011). *Sport and exercise psychology: A Canadian perspective*, 2nd ed. Toronto, Ontario: Pearson Canada.

Durand-Bush, N., Salmela, J. H., & Green-Demers, I. (2001). The Ottawa Mental Skills Assessment Tool (OMSAT-3). *The Sport Psychologist, 15*, 1–19.

Lane, A. M. (2008). *Sport and exercise psychology*. London: Hodder Education.

Mahoney, M. J. (1989). Psychological predictors of elite and non-elite performance in Olympic weightlifting. *International Journal of Sport Psychology, 20*, 1–12.

Mahoney, M. J., Gabriel, T. J., & Perkins, T. S. (1987). Psychological skills and exceptional athletic performance. *The Sport Psychologist, 1*, 181–199.

Smith, R. E., & Smoll, F. L. (1995). Development and validation of a multidimensional measure of sport-specific psychological skills: The Athletic Coping Skills Inventory-28. *Journal of Sport & Exercise Psychology, 17*, 370–398.

Thomas, P. R., Murphy, S. M., & Hardy, L. (1999). Test of Performance Strategies: Development and preliminary validation of a comprehensive measure of athletes' psychological skills. *Journal of Sports Sciences, 17*, 697–711.

Triplett, N. (1898). The dynamogenic factors in pacemaking and competition. *American Journal of Psychology, 9*, 507–533. http://psychclassics.yorku.ca/Triplett/

Weinberg, R. S., & Gould, D. (2010). *Foundations of sport and exercise psychology*, 5th ed. Champaign, IL: Human Kinetics.

Chapter 2

Achievement Motivation

Key Concepts and Theories

- Achievement goal theory
- Goal orientations
- Motivational climate
- Performance profiling
- Goal setting

On the Road, Again ...

While taking the train to training camp, Laura closes her eyes and begins to think about playing wheelchair basketball. Her mind wanders to images of the various successes she's had in her career. Memories begin flooding her mind, each as accurate and as vivid as they would be had they just happened yesterday:

- A much younger Laura, celebrating the first time she was able to generate enough power to successfully make a free-throw shot.
- Last training camp, where she finally beat Donna, her longtime teammate and biggest position-rival, in an all-out sprint on the court, and last,
- The plane ride home last season from the World Championships, overwhelmed with feelings of pride and accomplishment after realizing that she had hit her season performance goal of improving her shooting percentage by 7 percent.

"There is not a sport in the world that I would rather be playing. I can't wait to get to training camp," Laura says to herself, just before dozing off.

Introduction

Why do you strive for success in your sport? For many athletes, recalling past successes is a method to pump up, to elicit positive emotions, and/or to remind ourselves of why we love our sport. However, recalling and critically analyzing previous and subjective successes (and subjective failures, for that matter) can also provide you with an indication of what makes you tick, as it relates to your motivation

13

to pursue success in your sport. How you personally define success (and failure) in sport, in addition to how much you value skill mastery and how mentally tough you are, represent factors that contribute to a specific type of motivation called *achievement motivation*. Achievement motivation essentially refers to the degree of effort and commitment you have to pursuing success in your sport. Understanding the various factors that contribute to your own achievement motivation can provide insights into how much effort you are likely to put forth in a given situation, how resilient you may be in the face of adversity or failure, and how your perceived ability, self-confidence, and self-efficacy may be affected by personal successes and failures within your sport.

Defining Success and Failure in Sport

Consider how you, personally, define success and failure in sport. Of course, and especially in a performance domain such as sport, there is objective success and there is objective failure (i.e., winning and losing a competition, respectively). However, this may or may not be your *subjective* definition of success and failure in sport, or, it may represent only one aspect of your definition for these terms. For example, one of the successes that Laura recalls in the opening paragraph is gaining enough upper body strength to shoot a basketball the distance required to have a chance of successfully making a free-throw shot. This does not fit into the simplistic and objective definition of success. Laura did not win anything. Being able to generate enough strength to shoot a basketball 15 feet does not guarantee that the ball will even successfully fall into the basket, let alone guarantee a win. In this situation, Laura considers this personal accomplishment a success, and thus, it can be said that part of Laura's definition of success comprises achieving personal performance goals that are independent of winning in some way. Other possible conceptions of success in sport might include: being more successful than a teammate or opponent (even if you do not objectively win), fulfilling a coach's directives, making one's teammates laugh or feel supported, or perceiving that others are pleased with your performance. It is clear that success can be, for some, a multidimensional construct.

Similarly, one's definition of failure in sport may also be more complex than simply losing a competition. For example, an athlete may perceive failure if he or she fails to reach some performance standard with respect to the execution of a skill, feels outperformed by a teammate or opponent, or perceives he or she has disappointed the coach. Even if the team wins, the athlete may feel he or she has performed poorly compared to the previous performance. Note that these lists of *possible* conceptions of success and failure are not exhaustive and that every athlete will have an individually and experientially constructed definition of success and failure. It's even quite likely that two athletes belonging to the same sport team may have markedly different subjective definitions of success and of failure.

Understanding your own definitions of success and failure in sport can certainly help you understand your feelings and emotions before, during, and after a sport competition. Complete the Try It Out! Activity 1 on page 17 to get a better idea of your own subjective definitions of success and failure. As it relates to the use of mental skills, understanding your definitions of success and failure can allow you to more effectively structure performance enhancement programs that make use of mental skills and tools such as performance planning and routines, and goal setting. We will discuss goal setting later in this chapter, while performance planning and the use of routines will be discussed in Chapter 5.

In the training camp hotel, Laura and her roommate Shawna are laying on their beds, chatting about Donna (Laura's biggest position-rival):

Shawna: Hey, did you hear that Donna apparently trained with a personal trainer all off-season? She's gonna be so fit this season! That is going to help us out so huge this year.
Laura: Really? No, I didn't know that. Have you seen her? I mean, does she look more fit than I do?
S: Hmmm. I dunno. I mean, you guys probably look about the same, I guess.
L: I guess it's not a big deal. What matters is who beats who on the court, you know? That's what coach will be looking at, anyway. I just need to make sure I beat her at all of the drills and stuff.
S: [laughs] Yah, yah. I know. You are always all about beating other people!
L: [laughs] I know! But that's why I'm the best!

Your professor or course instructor has likely reviewed several theories which help us understand athletes' achievement motivation; however, arguably the most popular achievement motivation theory being examined in the sport psychology literature today is called the *achievement goal theory*. Goal orientations represent the achievement focus you tend to have when participating in sport and sport-related activities (e.g., competition, training, rehabilitation, practice, etc.). You can certainly see how your own personal definitions of success and failure will come into play here.

> ## Deep Thought
>
> Discuss how goal orientations are related to one's definitions of success and failure with a classmate, teammate, or friend. Here's a hint: the relationship will relate to the frequency of perceptions of success and failure experienced.

Let's briefly look at the two goal orientations. If you are an athlete who tends to be highly focused on personal improvement and personal mastery of your sport, then you are an athlete with a high task goal orientation. Conversely, if you are an athlete who defines success relative to whether, and how easily, you demonstrate superior skill and ability compared to an opponent, you are an athlete with a high ego goal orientation. Moreover, the goal orientations are considered to be orthogonal; the amount of one goal orientation does not influence the amount of the other goal orientation.

Here's a simple metaphor to explain this concept: Think about two jars, one holding only blue jelly beans and one holding only red jelly beans. Let's assume the jars collectively represent an athlete's achievement focus, blue jelly beans represent a task goal orientation, and red jelly beans represent an ego goal orientation.

Consequently, an athlete will have a certain number of blue jelly beans in her blue jelly bean jar and a certain number of red jelly beans in her red jelly bean jar. Notice how the number of blue jelly beans has no influence on how many red jelly beans there are. She could have two jars containing similar numbers of jelly beans, or, two jars containing different amounts of jelly beans. Similarly, an athlete will have a certain amount of task goal orientation and a certain amount of ego goal orientation. Generally, the amount of each goal orientation is quantified as high or low (e.g., an athlete might have a high task–high ego goal orientation 'profile').

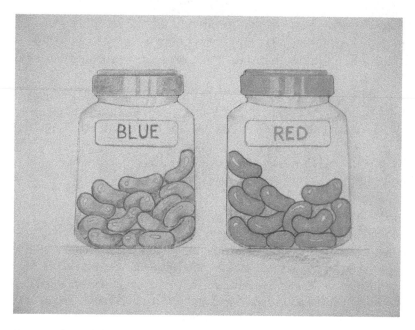

Courtesy of Daniel Gregg

If we review Shawna and Laura's conversation in vignette 2.2, we can gain some insight into Laura's predominant achievement goal orientation. In particular, pay attention to the part of the conversation where Shawna suggests that Laura is "always all about beating other people." Laura confirms this and suggests that beating others as her primary focus is what makes her highly successful in wheelchair basketball. Laura is probably high in ego goal orientation since it is clear that she, at least in part, defines success as demonstrating superiority over others. If you return to the chapter-opening vignette you can glean additional information regarding Laura's achievement focus; notice that both the task goal orientation (e.g., becoming strong enough to shoot the free throw distance, achieving a personal performance goal) and ego goal orientation (i.e., beating a playing position rival) are present. This would lead you to conclude that Laura has a high ego orientation but also some degree of task orientation, as well.

So what? you may be asking at this point in time. *So what if I can identify what my, or what my athlete's, achievement goal orientation profile is?* Although reviewing research findings is not the focus of this supplemental book, there is ample research evidence suggesting that the most adaptive athlete achievement goal profile (with regard to athlete success and continued participation) is one that is high task–high ego. This may seem surprising given some of the negative associations found to exist between high ego orientation and sport perceptions and experience, but the generally accepted explanation is that because high ego orientations are somewhat endemic in competitive sport (i.e., have a focus on winning and "being the best"), then pairing a high ego orientation with a high task orientation can serve to maintain an athlete's motivation and perceptions of self-efficacy and perceived competence in times where that athlete may be overmatched or simply not playing or performing well. This is not to say that we are suggesting that coaches promote or attempt to develop high ego orientations in their athletes. Most competitive athletes already possess a moderate, if not high, ego orientation and therefore placing a developmental emphasis on this orientation is likely not necessary or advantageous.

Complete Try It Out! Activity 2 on page 19 to determine your own levels of task- and ego-goal orientation.

Motivational Climate: How Others Can Influence Your Achievement Focus

As you have probably learned in your motivation lecture or from your course textbook, there are some personal and environmental factors that can directly influence which achievement goal orientation becomes most salient in a given sport situation or experience. Depending on how strong this influence is on you, it is possible that your dispositional tendency of being more task goal-oriented or more ego goal-oriented may be suppressed and the salience of the recessive goal orientation enhanced.

One such factor is the environment in which practice and/or competition occurs. More specifically, your coaches, trainers, and sometimes your sport's governing body, can dictate which achievement goal orientation becomes most emphasized in your practice, training, and competition environments. Interestingly, sometimes a coach's or team's coaching/playing philosophy can be inconsistent with the actual practice and training structure, coach behaviours, and verbal and nonverbal messages sent to athletes. A coach or team may express "on paper" that he, she, or they are athlete-centered and focused on individual athlete development and growth, but their actual achievement motivation orientation may be ego-focused (i.e., focused on winning or being the best). These types of inconsistencies can always be ascertained through observation of the various goal orientation–relevant performance and training structures, statements, and behaviours expressed by team leaders (e.g., coaches, management, captains, etc.). It is what is *actually expressed* during practice, training, and competition, *not* what is publicly advocated, that determines the achievement motivation-related environmental focus for an athlete or team.

In sport psychology terms, we call this achievement motivation-related environment that a coaching staff or organization creates for an athlete or group of athletes the *motivational climate*. If winning and beating others is emphasized by the coaching staff and the organization, an ego goal orientation is encouraged; however, if personal mastery and self-improvement are emphasized, a task goal orientation is encouraged. For example, if a coach *consistently* and *frequently* makes comments such as "we have to beat these guys next week," "we can't lose this game," "the only way to be the best is to beat the best," and the like, then that coach is intentionally or unintentionally fostering an ego-oriented sport environment: the focus is on beating others and demonstrating superiority through beating others. The motivational climate can also be task-oriented. For example, when coaches emphasize skill development and mastery, setting personal performance goals that are relative to one's own previous performances, and deemphasize the focus on winning (*Note:* this is not the same as deemphasizing the importance of winning!), a task-oriented motivational climate is evident.

Complete Try It Out! Activity 3 on page 21 to assess your own team's motivational climate and to determine which goal orientation your sport team is emphasizing to its athletes.

Try It Out!

Activity 1: How Do <u>You</u> Define "Success" and "Failure" in Your Sport?

Given what you have just learned about the individual nature of athletes' definitions of success and failure in sport, take a few minutes and write down your own personal definitions. Use the three or four performance memories you recalled earlier (and others, if needed) to help you.

For the memories that you recalled that were successes, understand that those memories will give you an idea of your own personal definition of success in sport. Similarly, your memories of your failures in sport will let you come up with a definition of failure in sport that is specific to you. Again, if you need to, recall some additional memories of successes and failures you've had in sport to help you construct your definitions.

We suggest you create a simple bullet-point list of your definition for success and failure, respectively. We have provided a template below. Think about your memories, and come up with general themes that represent what is happening in each memory. Then, put it in the success or failure list, accordingly. For example, in the opening scenario, Laura's memory of beating her teammate in an all-out sprint during training camp would be put in the "success" list. In terms of a general theme, she might choose to use "beating others" as the description to represent that memory.

Now you try it: Review and analyze your performance memories of success and failure. When you stop coming up with new general themes you can be pretty confident that you are finished with your definition, regardless of how many or how few bullet points you have.

<u>My definition of success in sport (add more or use fewer bullet points if needed)</u>:

-
-
-
-

<u>My definition of failure in sport (add more or use fewer bullet points if needed)</u>:

-
-
-

Try It Out!

Activity 2: What Are Your Levels of Task- and Ego-Goal Orientation?

Use your perceived successes and failures you identified in Try It Out! Activity 1 to help you determine whether you are more task-oriented or more ego-oriented when it comes to achievement goal orientation. You may also find it helpful to reflect on what really motivates you to participate in your sport with regards to practice, training, and competition.

Subjectively classify yourself as low, moderate, or high task goal-oriented, and low, moderate, or high ego goal-oriented (e.g., high task–low ego, low task–moderate ego, etc.). Provide a written explanation of why you believe that you have accurately classified yourself, giving examples and evidence from your sport experiences and cognitions.

Try It Out!

Activity 3: What Motivational Climate Is Your Coach/Coaching Staff Creating?

Now that you have a strong understanding of motivation climate in sport, identify which achievement motivation focus your coach or coaching staff *says* they promote in their program (i.e., what they *publicly* advocate):

Provide a brief summary of how they typically explain this focus to prospective athletes or interested parties (e.g., "we are all about the athlete," "our number-one priority is developing your skills," etc.):

List as many achievement motivation-related behaviours or cognitions you can recall being *consistently* expressed by your coach or coaching staff during sport (e.g., verbal emphasis on beating the other team, throwing clipboards when we lose, setting individual performance goals, praising personal improvements in performance, etc.):

Hopefully, the behaviour and cognitions you listed <u>match</u> the achievement motivation focus you identified above. If not, this can confuse, annoy, and perhaps even de-motivate athletes if they are lead to expect one type of sport performance focus, but get another.

Putting It All Together

What Can Be Done to Help Athletes Focus on the Task Orientation?

Although there are many different ways in which you can encourage a task orientation focus with athletes, we've chosen to present two strategies that are commonly used by sport psychologists, coaches, and athletes: performance profiling and goal setting. We recommend that these two strategies be used in tandem, completing the performance profile first, which is then used to inform and even guide the goal-setting process.

Performance Profiling

One way to encourage a task-oriented achievement motivation focus is to complete performance profiling with an athlete at regular intervals. Performance profiling is a tool that sport psychologists and coaches often employ to identify an athlete's performance strengths and weaknesses. Though all use the same general structure, there are several different variations of performance profiling, and we encourage you to experiment with different ones to find the variation that works best for you or your athletes.

The variation we are reviewing here encourages the athlete to come up with an exhaustive list of qualities possessed by the most successful athlete he or she has seen compete regularly in his or her sport, whereas other popular variations limit the athlete to a list of five to ten qualities. Typically, athletes will create lists in the five- to ten-item range, whether limited to five to ten items or not. However, we believe that *not* imposing a limit may help reduce any anxiety the athletes may feel should they think the administrator is looking for a correct number of responses. Athletes are given as much time as they need to complete the list, and they are reminded that there are no incorrect responses. If the athlete has trouble identifying qualities, they can be reprompted to think of the physical and psychological qualities possessed by the "best" athlete they know or have seen play in their sport.

Once the athletes believe their lists are complete, they are asked to rank-order the various qualities in terms of their influence on sport performance, with the most important quality ranked 1, second most important ranked 2, and so on, until all qualities are ranked. It may be necessary to remove certain items from one's list, primarily those items that are not actually amenable to change following deliberate practice. As an example, confidence, focus, strength, and speed are all qualities (the first two psychological, the latter two physical) that can be improved following systematic, regular, and committed practice. But qualities such as height, gender, and geographical location cannot be changed through deliberate practice. If you choose to remove any items from your athlete's list, be sure to explain why you are doing so. If needed, allow the athlete more time to complete this task. It is also important to refrain from projecting your own opinions of what the most and least important qualities are into your athletes' rankings—it is *their* list, after all, not yours.

After the rank ordering is completed, athletes are then asked to rate their own level of performance at each of the qualities in their list. It is important here to tell the athletes that you would like them to rate their average level of performance of each quality (i.e., how "good" they are at that quality, in general, or, on most days). We recommend using a 0–10 point scale so that you can establish a true midpoint (i.e., 5 is typically considered to be the middle on a 10-point scale, but if the scale is from 1–10, a rating of 5 is above the actual true midpoint). If the athletes are struggling with ranking any particular quality, assist them by suggesting they compare their level of performance at that particular quality to that of the "best athlete they know in their sport." A sample performance profile is presented in Figure 2.1, below.

Qualities of ___Mike T.___, the best athlete I know in my sport that I have competed against	Rank order of quality (Where '1' = most important to success in my sport)	My rating of myself, compared to ___Mike T.___ ('0' = I am very weak at this quality; '10' = I have the perfect amount of this quality for my sport)
Confident all the time	2	7
~~Strength~~		
Stays calm all the time	1	2
Always focused	3	5
~~Speed~~		
Always seems to be having fun	4	3

Once this last step is completed, your athlete has completed his or her performance profile. What you now have is a highly individualized list of the strengths and weaknesses of your athlete. This list can be used, not only to identify these strengths and weaknesses, but also to more specifically track athlete development over time, such as by conducting performance profiling at regular intervals (e.g., once a month). In addition, a well-administered performance profile can allow a sport psychologist or coach to accurately identify the qualities needing the most improvement (i.e., the qualities that are *most negatively* affecting a given athlete's performance). These qualities can then be targeted through deliberate practice, which we highly recommend pairing with goal setting, discussed in the next section of this chapter. This type of targeted deliberate practice will give athletes the "most bang" for their training "buck"; by targeting the weakest areas that are most strongly related to performance, the athlete will experience the greatest performance gains.

Try It Out! Create your own performance profile. Use this overview to help you structure your performance profile and be as honest as possible when rating yourself on the various characteristics you identify as contributing significantly to performance in your sport.

Goal Setting

Your professor or course instructor has probably noted that goal setting is one of the most used psychological skills in sport. When employed *appropriately*, it is also one of the most effective psychological skills to increase effort, focus, and task persistence. We recommend pairing goal setting as a follow-up program to any sport performance assessment, such as that derived from performance profiling. If you can increase effort, focus, and task persistence during training and practice periods you will come closer to optimizing training and practice results. A good goal-setting program can help you accomplish this.

Most athletes will tell you that they set goals for their sport. What you should really be interested in, however, is whether they are using *effective* goal-setting techniques, and, if you are a coach or group leader, whether you are *facilitating* that process. Arguably, setting "any old goal" may be better than not setting any goal at all, but "any old goal" may or may not be effective at influencing sport performance. Certainly, much research has been conducted on goal setting in sport, and we now have a fairly good understanding of what makes for an effective (and ineffective) goal-setting program. Some guidelines are outlined below.

1. **Understand that goals are not magical.** Simply setting a goal to be the fastest sprinter on your track team does not mean that your Type II muscle fibers will miraculously increase in size overnight and without any effort on your part. In addition, simply setting an outcome goal does not guarantee that you will know *how* to make that goal a reality. The point that is being made here is that it is important for athletes to distinguish between goals and wishes. We all wish for success in sport, or for specific accomplishments or accolades. We don't all set *goals*—or at least, not effectively. Effectively structured and well-implemented goal-setting programs produce highly performance-affective results. They also require hard work and regular review.

2. **Set outcome, performance, and process goals.** Outcome goals are more commonly known by the general population as "long–term" or "dream" goals. These are the goals that you want to accomplish when all is said and done. For example, an athlete may set a goal to win an Olympic gold medal, to make the high school basketball team, or to win a given golf tournament. Outcome goals typically require social comparison: one's performance is compared to that of at least one other person. Performance goals focus on achieving personal and highly controllable performance standards, regardless of what other competitors or teammates are doing. For example, shaving 2/10 of a second off of a front crawl swim time is a performance goal because it involves meeting a personal standard and it is highly controllable (i.e., other competitors have little direct influence on whether one achieves this goal).

   Goals that involve personal standards *but* have relatively low controllability typically have some aspect of social comparison to it, and thus are better categorized as outcome goals (e.g., finishing above the 85th percentile for an upcoming marathon, in order to achieve a "personal best" finish). Process goals focus an athlete on task-relevant behaviours, information, strategies, and procedures that are related to performance execution. For example, the swimmer who set a performance goal of shaving 2/10 of a second off of his front crawl swim time for a given race could set a process goal to focus on his breathing before that race to help control his anxiety symptoms. Controlling anxiety will have a positive influence on his performance, thus, focusing on breathing is a strategy that will help the swimmer perform better. Therefore, as a result of implementing a task-relevant process goal, the swimmer will be in a better position to achieve his performance goal. Other process goals could involve identifying information that the swimmer needs to attend to during the race (e.g., the starter's gun/buzzer, the wall) as well as procedures the swimmer could follow to increase his chances of success (e.g., executing a pre-performance routine).

It is strongly recommended that athletes set all three types of goals. Setting only outcome goals does not make for effective goal setting. Imagine if you set a goal to restore a classic car but did not have the faintest idea about the *particular parts* of the car that needed to be worked on or regarding *how* to actually restore each part. The goal of restoring that classic car would likely not be achieved. The same idea applies to sport-related goals. If you identify only where you want to finish, you'll have no idea where to start or even how to move forward toward the finish line.

If you set *only* performance goals, you wouldn't know how to most effectively and/or efficiently go about achieving these performance goals as you would not have laid out a specific plan of attack. What can happen in these situations is that athletes either wear themselves out trying anything and everything to achieve the performance goal (i.e., trial-and-error approach) or become de-motivated to pursue the goal because they become overwhelmed with all of the possible options regarding where to start. Last, if athletes set *only* process goals, motivation (and thus task effort, focus, and persistence) may falter as they may not understand the "bigger picture" —*why* they need to work at the process goals, or, what accomplishing the process goals will set them up for in the near and/or more distant future.

3. **Set goals for training/practice and competition.** It is, perhaps, much easier for athletes to get motivated to work hard, stay focused, and persevere in competition than in training and practice sessions. In addition to setting goals for competition, athletes should also be encouraged to set goals pertaining to training and practice in order to clearly define expectations regarding behaviours, attitudes, and effort during these periods.

4. **Make your goals a "to-do" list, not a "to-don't" list.** Using negatively stated goals can encourage a failure-avoidance goal orientation (being focused on avoiding failure is thought to produce inferior performance results as opposed to being focused on achieving success). For example, a goal stated as: "Reduce your goals-against-average to 2.50" focuses a hockey goalie on not letting goals into the net (i.e., not failing). This same goal could be changed to: "Increase save percentage to 0.900," which would focus the goalie on making more saves (i.e., being successful). Although these goals may sound extremely similar, they can affect goalies differentially. The prior may conjure negative images and a focus on goals being scored against them. The latter can elicit positive images with a focus on blocking shots.

5. **Structure each goal effectively.** The most well-known goal-structuring method is dubbed SMART goal setting. This acronym stands for specific, measurable, adjustable, realistic, and time-based. All goals should follow this goal structure—whether they are outcome, performance, or process goals. Goals should be as specific as possible. For example, instead of a volleyball setter having a goal to "make the Olympic volleyball team," she should have a goal to "make the Olympic volleyball team as the second-string setter." The latter identifies position as well as role. This makes expectations of goal attainment clearer to the athlete.

Goals should also be measurable. Sometimes this is easily accomplished, especially with outcome goals. For example, in the previous volleyball example, goal attainment is measurable because the volleyball player will either make the team, or she will not. However, performance and process goals also need to be measurable. A basketball player who sets a performance goal to "improve his vertical jump" will achieve this goal if he improves his vertical jump *by any amount* (e.g., improving by 1/16 of an inch is still an improvement!). Thus, you can see why it is crucial to define what will be considered successful attainment by quantifying the goal. For example, the revised goal statement of: "improve vertical jump by 3.5 inches" makes it very clear that goal pursuit will not be considered a success unless the athlete improves his vertical jump by at least 3.5 inches.

Next, athletes should be aware that their goals can be adjusted up or down, *when appropriate*. This goal-setting tenet should not be misinterpreted. This is *not* designed to allow athletes to adjust goals due to a lack of effort, focus, or persistence. These adjustments are only acceptable when something *outside of the athlete's control* impedes goal pursuit (e.g., injury or illness) or when the goal is achieved sooner than anticipated (e.g., the goal was too easy or the athlete worked extremely hard). The adjustability factor of SMART goal setting is not intended to give an athlete an easy out for a goal to which they have committed pursuit.

Goals should also be realistic. The determination of what is realistic should be based on objective evaluations of an athlete's goal-relevant personal factors and current level of performance. For example, the goal of a high school football player returning to full practice after suffering a major knee injury may be unrealistic if he plans to run the 40-yard dash in his pre-injury time. This is not to say that goals should be easy, in fact, the most effective goals are those that are subjectively considered moderately difficult. This means athletes must perceive that they will have to work very hard to achieve the goal, but also that they, in no way, believe the goal is impossible to reach.

Finally, goals must be time-based. Going back to the basketball player's vertical jump goal, if no deadline for goal attainment was set, the athlete could take as long as he wanted to reach that goal, and it would still be considered a successful goal pursuit. However, more often than not, goals need to be achieved in some timely manner in order for the goal pursuer to reap the maximum benefit from the pursuit. For example, perhaps the basketball player had an outcome goal of obtaining a college scholarship. If there was no time deadline on achieving the vertical jump goal, it is possible that the athlete may achieve the goal too late for it to be considered by potential college scouts. Additionally, setting a time deadline mobilizes effort in athletes. If you know that something is 'due' by a certain date, you are much more likely to do the work required to meet that deadline, compared to when there is no deadline in sight.

6. **Track goal pursuit progress and evaluate goal pursuit outcomes regularly.** Recording goals on paper and displaying them where they can be seen on a regular, if not daily, basis (e.g., on the fridge, in a locker, etc.) is a great way to keep athletes focused on the things that they need to do in order to be successful. In addition, having athletes keep weekly goal progress logs is another way to increase the effectiveness of a goal-setting program. With the many advances in technology in the last decade, goal progress logs no longer need to be of the paper-and-pencil variety. For example, athletes may create a log that is regularly updated and saved to a word processing or spreadsheet program, sport psychologists or coaches may choose to make use of certain social media utilities (e.g., have athletes report weekly goal progress on group pages or forums), or, mobile text messaging may be used to report weekly progress toward goals. As an added bonus, athletes may be more motivated to complete progress logs if contemporary collection methods, such as the use of social media or mobile text messaging, are employed.

It is also important to evaluate the effectiveness of athletes' goal pursuits regularly. This serves to maintain or increase motivation toward goal-setting program adherence by demonstrating to the athlete that the program is working (i.e., performance gains are observable). This requires the coach or sport psychologist to provide the athlete with either statistical (performance numbers) or anecdotal (performance examples) evidence of changes in performance. An alternative approach is to have the athletes reflect on their own performance changes since the initiation of the goal-setting program (or since the last evaluation). The key is to link any performance gains to goal pursuit behaviours, wherever links are evident (i.e., do not mislead your athletes by fabricating links that do not exist). Regular goal-setting program evaluation may also identify goals that are not "working" or that need to be adjusted.

7. **Support your athlete(s) in their goal pursuits.** Being aware of what goals your athletes have set for themselves can go a long way toward increasing goal-setting program adherence and motivation. Knowing what your athletes' goals are will allow you to tailor feedback during practice, training, and competition such that they relate to various goals in their goal-setting program. This will assist your athletes with their goal pursuits through provision of goal-related instructional feedback and/or goal-focusing reminders. As well, you may also be able to maintain or even increase goal-setting program adherence and motivation via the provision of goal-related motivational feedback. In addition to ensuring that you are aware of your athletes' goals, it is also beneficial to educate family or friends, or other supporters, of your athletes' goals so that they, too, can tailor any feedback (ideally, primarily motivational in nature).

Try it out! Create your own goal-setting program, while doing your best to follow the guidelines reviewed above. Select one outcome goal that you would like to achieve in the next six to eight months. To help you reach this outcome goal, set two or three performance goals. To help you reach each performance goal, set two or three process goals. Once you are done, check for goal consistency and relevance, that is, each process goal (if performed consistently) should contribute to your attainment of its corresponding performance goal. The attainment of each performance goal should contribute to your attainment of your outcome goal. You can see that when your goals are structured in this way, you really need to focus your efforts only on consistently performing/achieving your process goals. This is great news as process goals are stated in behavioural terms (i.e., they are "action goals") and are the goals with the greatest degree of personal control.

Summary: Putting It All Together

This chapter has discussed the importance of not just knowing what achievement motivation is, but, more importantly, knowing the value in understanding *your* achievement motivation as well as how you define success and failure. It is important to work to move away from the "black-and-white" or dichotomous definitions of success and failure (i.e., win = success; lose = failure) as this conceptualization of success and failure can lead to very negative influences on your thoughts, feelings, and attitude toward your sport! Think of it this way: as an athlete, you will achieve many more failures than you will successes if you define success *only* as winning. Allow yourself to experience pride and a sense of accomplishment more often by working toward a more individualized and a more multidimensional definition of success and failure. Once you determine what success and failure really mean to you, complete a performance profile to identify your strengths and weaknesses and then construct a goal-setting program *that is consistent with your personal definitions of success* to guide your thoughts, feelings, and behaviours within your sport.

Suggested Readings and References

Cury, F., Elliot, A. J., Sarrazin, P., Da Fonseca, D., & Rufo, M. (2002). The trichotomous achievement goal model and intrinsic motivation: A sequential mediational analysis. *Journal of Experimental Social Psychology, 38,* 473–481.

Duda, J. L. (2001). Achievement goal research in sport: Pushing the boundaries and clarifying some misunderstandings. In G. C. Roberts (Ed.), *Advances in motivation in sport and exercise.* Champaign, IL: Human Kinetics.

Elliot, A. J., Cury, F., Fryer, J. W., & Huguet, P. (2006). Achievement goals, self-handicapping, and performance attainment: A mediational analysis. *Journal of Sport & Exercise Psychology, 28,* 344–361.

Elliot, A. J., & McGregor, H. A. (2001). A 2 × 2 achievement goal framework. *Journal of Personality and Social Psychology, 80,* 501–519.

Harter, S. (1999). *The construction of self.* New York: Guilford.

Nicholls, J. G. (1984). Achievement motivation: Conceptions of ability, subjective experience, task choice, and performance. *Psychological Review, 91,* 328–346.

Nicholls, J. G. (1989). *The competitive ethos and democratic education.* Cambridge, MA: Harvard University Press.

Nien, C-L., & Duda, J. L. (2007). The effect of situationally emphasized achievement goals and win/loss on engagement in a cycle ergometer task. *Journal of Sports Sciences, 25,* 320.

Roberts, G. C. (2001). Understanding the dynamics of motivation in physical activity: The influence of achievement goals on motivational processes. In G. C. Roberts (Ed.), *Advances in motivation in sport and exercise* (pp. 1–50). Champaign, IL: Human Kinetics.

Weinberg, R. S., & Gould, D. (2007). *Foundations of sport and exercise psychology* (4th ed.), Champaign, IL: Human Kinetics.

Weiner, B. (1986). *An attribution theory of achievement motivation and emotion.* New York: Springer.

Williams. J. M. (2010). *Applied sport psychology: Personal growth to peak performance* (6th ed.). New York, NY: McGraw-Hill.

Chapter 3

Confidence and Efficacy Beliefs

Key Concepts and Theories

- Self-efficacy theory
- Collective efficacy (you may also want to skip ahead to Chapter 9 on group dynamics)
- Confidence as a state versus a trait

Moving On Up...

Ashley, a grade 11 student, plays on several teams at her high school: volleyball, basketball, badminton, curling, and soccer. She's had quite a lot of success at all of these sports at the high school level, but she knows that she needs to start focusing on one or two sports in order to compete at the Canada Games and have coaches notice her for their university programs. Ashley has spent some time talking to her school guidance counsellor, parents, and coaches, for their advice on how to decide what sport she should focus on.

At a high school basketball tournament, the coach of the regional competitive club team invites Ashley to try out for the team. It goes so well that the coach offers her a place on the team. He tells her he thinks she has the potential to be a starter on his team, and with some hard work, will be able to earn a position on a university team when she graduates from high school.

Key Concepts Related to Confidence

When we think about the qualities that make an athlete successful, oftentimes confidence is one of the first that comes to mind. Indeed, confidence is widely considered to be one of the most important psychological factors for determining how successful an athlete will be. Confidence is also a term that can have many different meanings; that is, there are different types of confidence. In this chapter we will explore some of the different types of confidence as well as how you can apply theory and research in order to increase an athlete's or exerciser's confidence.

One of the key concepts surrounding confidence is that it is a construct that is **multidimensional** in nature. What does this mean? Confidence can take different forms, depending on the individual and the specific situation. For example, what areas of your life are you highly confident about? Which ones are you not as confident about? How do you feel about your sport abilities? What about abilities for specific sports? What about your overall level of confidence as an individual? Chances are you were able to identify some areas, or domains, where you are more confident than others. As well, you may have thought about specific situations that make you more or less confident. Ashley, the athlete from our profile, may be very confident in her free-throw abilities in basketball, but she may be less confident about her ability to perform a new defensive pattern with her new team. Using examples from your own life, explain the difference between:

- State confidence versus trait confidence
- Sport-specific confidence versus global self-confidence

Regardless of whether we are discussing global self-confidence or sport-specific confidence, research has shown that confidence is associated with performance. Athletes with higher levels of confidence tend to perform at a higher level than those with low confidence. Why do you think confidence is such an essential element for successful performance?

Our confidence influences our thoughts, feelings, and actions. As you probably discussed in class, factors such as anxiety, motivation, focus, attributions, and use of psychological skills are all related to our confidence levels. Essentially, confidence can be a self-fulfilling prophecy. The belief that you can succeed can have a profound effect on how you approach the situation, cope with stressors, execute your performance, and interpret the outcome of your efforts. Complete Try It Out! Activity 1 on page 37 to create a concept map showing how confidence is related to other concepts.

Self-Efficacy

Think of self-efficacy as a very specific form of confidence. According to Bandura (1997), self-efficacy refers to someone's belief in his or her ability to complete a specific behaviour in a specific situation. This is different from the concept of outcome expectancies (i.e., our expectations about the consequences of our actions). How would you explain the difference between the two concepts to a young athlete? Think of an example that shows the difference between the two concepts and that a young athlete can relate to.

Bandura's (1997) self-efficacy theory is the most commonly used explanation for how we develop our self-efficacy beliefs. The strength of our self-efficacy beliefs comes from four specific sources: previous mastery experiences, vicarious experiences (e.g., imagery and modeling), verbal persuasion, and affective and physiological states. Try It Out! Activity 2 on page 39 will help you to explore strategies for building self-efficacy.

Self-Efficacy in Exercise

Confidence and self-efficacy are important concepts outside sport-related settings. They are also key factors in understanding people's exercise behaviour. Within the exercise psychology literature, often researchers examine different types of self-efficacy and how they are related to someone's ability to start and stick with an exercise program. The three types of self-efficacy often examined are task efficacy (i.e., completing specific exercises), coping efficacy (i.e., dealing with challenges to remaining active), and scheduling efficacy (i.e., planning and fitting exercise into our schedules). In Try It Out! Activity 3 on page 41, we will return to Ashley's scenario and her challenge of incorporating a new training program into her already busy schedule. For a more in-depth examination of how self-efficacy and confidence can factor into exercise adherence, take a look at Chapter 12 on physical activity later in this book.

Related Concepts

Many other concepts are similar, but distinct, from confidence. For example, confidence, self-efficacy, competence, self-concept, self-worth, and self-esteem may all sound as though they reflect similar feelings. Although all of these concepts reflect our beliefs about ourselves, there are some subtle differences between them. Test your knowledge by filling in the table shown in Try It Out! Activity 4 on page 43.

Collective Efficacy

Now that you have examined confidence and self-efficacy as they relate to an individual's beliefs, let's consider how these concepts can also operate at the group level. For example, Ashley may be confident in her abilities as a basketball player, but what about her team as a whole? Is the team confident in their ability to play as a group and reach their team goals for the season? As you may have discussed in class, Bandura's (1997) self-efficacy theory also discusses the concept of collective efficacy. This refers to the group's belief about their capabilities as a whole, not simply the sum of the individual group member's beliefs about their own abilities.

Deep Thought

Why is the sum or average of an individual team member's beliefs a poor measure of collective efficacy? Think about the last team you played on. Was the entire team on the same page in terms of confidence? Do players who are highly confident in their own abilities always play well and achieve success as a team? Why or why not? Discuss your thoughts with a partner.

Indeed, we can likely find many examples of how a "dream team" comprised of very skilled individual players do not function as well as a team of less-skilled players who work very well together as a group. As a result, the "dream team" players may all be highly confident in their own individual abilities but may doubt their ability to win as a team—leading them to have a low sense of collective efficacy.

Deep Thought

Watch a sports program, or check out a sports news publication or website. Look at the athlete and coach interviews. What words do they use to represent the idea of collective efficacy and how it influences their team's performance? Find specific examples of coaches, players, or management where they talk about collective efficacy. Notice how players may use words such as "I," "me," and "my" to talk about their own performance but use "we," "our," or "the team" to discuss the overall result of a game.

Similar to self-efficacy, there are various factors that are related to a team's collective efficacy and its subsequent performance. To explore the concepts that are related to collective efficacy, complete Try

It Out! Activity 5 on page 45. You may notice that it's a repeat of Try It Out! Activity 1. You can then compare whether the factors that are related to self-efficacy are the same or different when compared with those related to collective efficacy.

Summary: Putting It All Together

At this point, you have a good understanding of what confidence, self-efficacy, and collective efficacy are, as well as the factors that influence them. The next step is to develop strategies to help build a player, exerciser, or team's perception of their confidence. In order to do this, consider the different theories used in your class to explain how confidence and/or efficacy beliefs are developed. For example, Bandura's (1997) self-efficacy theory dictates that previous mastery experiences are the strongest source of self-efficacy (and collective efficacy). Therefore, if we wanted to boost an athlete's or team's self-efficacy going into a championship game, one option might be to create a highlight tape showing their previous wins against the same team they will play in the championship game. To help you put all that you've learned about efficacy together, complete the Putting It all Together Activity on page 47 to help Ashley's team improve their efficacy heading into playoffs.

Try It Out!

Activity 1: Map It Out!

Based on what you have learned so far about sport psychology, draw a concept map that reflects the other psychological concepts related to confidence. Note whether each is positively or negatively associated with confidence. To get you started, use the template below and then add to it. Notice that for some concepts, the relationship with confidence can be reciprocal (e.g., confidence and performance) rather than flowing in only one direction.

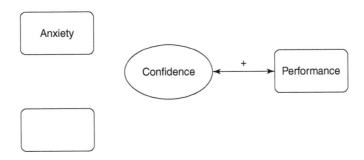

Activity 2: From Theory to Practice

Use Bandura's (1997) self-efficacy theory, or another theory used in class, to explain how confidence is developed. Draw a diagram showing the key concepts in the theory. Based on Ashley's example, what are some strategies she can use to boost her confidence going into an important basketball game? Make sure each of your strategies is related to the concepts within your chosen theory.

My theory is: _____

Diagram of concepts in my chosen theory:

Strategies Ashley can use to boost her confidence before an important game:

1.

2.

3.

4.

5.

Activity 3: Matching Challenges to Types of Self-Efficacy

Let's return to Ashley's scenario…

Ashley is pumped that she made the regional basketball team, but has noticed that the training schedule is much more rigorous than her high school team's schedule. She has also noticed that her fitness level is a bit lower than the other girls' fitness levels. The team has a strength and conditioning coach who has designed a training program for each player. Ashley's program requires her to go for a run three times a week and to do her resistance and plyometric training routine twice a week. The exercises are fairly new to her and she is worried about how she will find the time to fit training in on top of her homework, other school activities, and the additional travel time to the regional team's practices and games.

A. Identify specific challenges Ashley may have to contend with. Which type of efficacy is needed to overcome each of the challenges?

B. Based on what you know about the sources of self-efficacy, what strategies could Ashley use to increase her task, coping, and scheduling efficacy? Make sure your strategies are related to specific components of self-efficacy theory.

Activity 4: Differentiating between Similar Concepts

Based on what you have learned in class, try to illustrate the difference between the following concepts. Use examples from your own life or use Ashley's scenario to create examples.

Concept	Definition	Related Theory	Example
Confidence			
Self-efficacy			
Self-esteem			
Self-concept			
Competence			

Activity 5: Map It Out! Part II.

Based on what you have learned so far about sport psychology, draw a concept map that reflects the other psychological concepts related to collective efficacy. Note whether each is positively or negatively associated with collective efficacy. To get you started, use the template below and then add to it. Notice that for some concepts, the relationship can be reciprocal (e.g., collective efficacy and performance) rather than flowing in only one direction. Consider factors related to the individual players (e.g., task cohesion) as well as environmental factors (e.g., motivational climate), and sport factors (e.g., level of interdependence required by players, such as on a golf team vs. a basketball team).

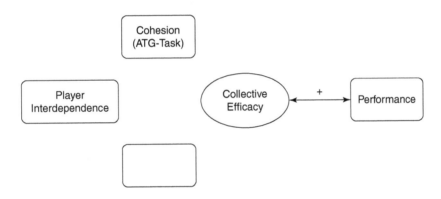

Putting It All Together

Let's consider Ashley's situation one last time:

Ashley's basketball team has been doing very well this season, but recently hit a slump. They are among the top three teams in the league, but have lost their last three games to teams that are ranked in the middle and bottom of the league. This has taken a toll on the team's confidence. The sudden-death playoff games start next week.

If you were Ashley's coach, what could you do to build the team's collective efficacy? Using the theory and research discussed in class, identify five team-based strategies and five individual strategies you would use as a coach. For each strategy, explain how it is based on either a theory (e.g., self-efficacy theory) or research finding (e.g., MG-M imagery increases confidence).

	Individual Athlete Strategies for Self-Efficacy	Team Strategies for Collective Efficacy
1.		
2.		
3.		
4.		
5.		

Suggested Readings and References

Bandura, A. (1997). *Self-efficacy: The exercise of control*. New York: Freeman.

Crocker, P. R. E. (2011). *Sport and exercise psychology: A Canadian perspective* (2nd ed.). Toronto, Canada: Pearson.

Lox, C. L., Martin Ginis, K. A., & Petruzzello, S. J. (2010). *The psychology of exercise: Integrating theory and practice* (3rd ed.). Scottsdale, AZ: Holcolm Hathaway.

Weinberg, R. S., & Gould, D. (2007). *Foundations of sport and exercise psychology* (4th ed.), Champaign, IL: Human Kinetics.

Chapter 4

Regulating Activation and Anxiety

Key Concepts and Theories

- The difference between arousal, anxiety, and stress
- Measurement of arousal and anxiety
- The matching hypothesis
- Techniques to help deal with somatic anxiety
- Techniques to help deal with cognitive anxiety
- How to apply multimodal techniques to reduce athletic anxiety

Coping with Challenges

Joe is a professional hockey player in the National Hockey League (NHL). Joe has had a successful career with the NHL team but is finding it challenging to meet the physical and psychological demands of continuing to play at this higher level. He is one of the oldest players on the team and is starting to question whether he can keep up with the younger players and if his playing days are about done. Joe finds himself getting incredibly nervous before games. Not only is he noticing his heart racing inexplicably, but his mind tends to be in overdrive in practice and also before, during, and after games. Consequently, his constant rumination is impeding his ability to perform optimally. He realizes he has only one or possibly two seasons left and is looking for help to ensure that he leaves on a high note.

What Are Arousal, Anxiety, and Stress?

Athletes and coaches often use the words *arousal, anxiety,* and *stress* interchangeably. Although the terms are similar, it is important to briefly review each term's definition to better understand how to develop interventions to help athletes. As you may recall, arousal is defined as "physiological activation or autonomic reactivity" (Gould & Krane, 1992, p.120). Arousal is a combination of physiological and psychological activation that lies on a continuum from low (e.g., deep sleep) to high (e.g., intense excitement). Arousal is a form of undifferentiated bodily energy (i.e., neither pleasant nor unpleasant) and can occur for both negative and positive events.

In contrast, anxiety is thought to be a negatively charged emotional state that is accompanied by worrying, fear, and high arousal. In Crocker's (2007) textbook entitled *Sport Psychology: A Canadian Perspective,* there is a good review of the three distinctions—trait and state anxiety, global and situation-specific, and cognitive and somatic anxiety—made by sport researchers when discussing anxiety and athletic performance. As such, we do not go into detail on those topics but encourage readers to review the key concepts prior to reading this chapter. We will briefly review two key aspects of athletic anxiety—cognitive and somatic—as they are a major focal point of the intervention section of this chapter. Cognitive anxiety is the mental component of anxiety and is caused by negative expectations about success or negative self-evaluation. An example would be if before a big game Joe is worrying about failing and has negative thoughts about his ability to perform. On the other hand, somatic anxiety is concerned with the physiological elements of the anxiety experience that develops directly from autonomic arousal. An example would be if Joe has an increase in his heart rate, sweaty hands, or tense muscles.

Several variables have been found to be linked to an athlete's anxiety level. Self-confidence has been found to play a key role in an athlete's performance. In fact, it has been suggested that, based on the finding that an athlete's self-confidence better predicts performance than somatic or cognitive anxiety, self-confidence may act as a protective factor against cognitive anxiety (see Chapter 3 on confidence for recommendations on how to bolster this important psychological trait). Additional factors linked to an athlete's anxiety levels are: personality, experience, skill level, gender, coping skills, goals and expectations to name a few. For example, some researchers have found gender differences when examining the relationship between cognitive and somatic anxiety and self-confidence. Specifically, Jones, Swain, and Cale (1991) found that female cognitive anxiety and self-confidence were determined by readiness to perform and the importance women personally placed on doing well. In contrast, the researchers found among males, cognitive and somatic anxieties were more strongly affected by their perception of their opponent's ability and the probability of winning. These results highlight the fact that it would be useful to consider several variables when developing a program to help athletes with their anxiety.

Deep Thought

How do you respond to a stressful situation? Think of a recent event that was stressful in your life. Using the definitions of *arousal, anxiety*, and *stress* describe how your body and mind responded to the situation. Were you anxious? Excited? Did your muscles tense up? Was your mind racing? Did your heart rate increase? Was there a change in respiration rate? Did you experience self-doubt? Try to analyze exactly how your mind and body respond to stressful events to gain a better understanding of the terminology and of yourself.

Lastly, stress is defined as a perceived imbalance between what is required to be successful in an important situation and what the individual perceives his or her ability is to meet the conditions. Anxiety and stress are created by the awareness of arousal. Thus, an athlete's *interpretation* of his or her arousal is pivotal to performance. In fact, research suggests that arousal can have either a debilitative or a facilitative effect on performance depending on how it is perceived by an athlete. An example of a facilitative approach to anxiety can be seen in the following quote by Tiger Woods: "The challenge is hitting good golf shots when you have to . . . to do it when the nerves are fluttering, the heart pounding, the palms sweating . . . that's the thrill" (Davies, 2001). This quote underlines how it is useful for athletes to view precompetitive arousal as a sign of excitement rather than anxiety.

Measuring Arousal and Anxiety

Sport psychology researchers and consultants can measure arousal and anxiety either subjectively or objectively. The most common method is subjective, that is self-report questionnaires. Some popular arousal activation questionnaires are the Activation-Deactivation Adjective Checklist (ADACL; Thayer, 1967) and the Somatic Perception Questionnaire (SPQ; Landy & Stern, 1971). There are several different self-report questionnaires available when measuring the different types of anxiety. Competitive trait anxiety is predominantly measured using two self-report questionnaires: Sport Competition Anxiety Test (SCAT; Martens, 1977) and the Sport Anxiety Scale (SAS; Smith, Smoll, & Schutz, 1990). The SAS is divided into cognitive (combined subscales of concentration and worry) and somatic anxiety. Competitive state anxiety is measured subjectively using the Competitive Sport Anxiety Inventory-2 (CSAI-2; Martens, Burton, Vealey, Bump, & Smith, 1990). This questionnaire has three subscales: cognitive anxiety, somatic anxiety, and self-confidence.

Research has shown the above-mentioned questionnaires to be both valid and reliable measures of arousal and anxiety and as such have been used in both the research and applied domain of sport psychology. Having athletes evaluate their somatic and cognitive anxiety, be it trait or state, is an important first step for sport psychology consultants working with an athlete. Self-awareness is key to helping athletes reach their potentials. However, it is important to note that self-report measures do have their limitations. Athletes will sometimes respond in a socially desirable manner skewing the results. To overcome this limitation, it helps to ask the athlete verbally to elaborate with specific examples.

Unfortunately, all too often when athletes are asked how their minds and bodies respond to stressful situations, the answer is frequently "I don't know." Luckily, objective measures are available that can be used in conjunction with the above-mentioned subjective measures to paint a clearer picture of how an athlete responds to stress both cognitively and somatically. For example, one can measure an athlete's heart rate, respiration rate, muscle tension, temperature, skin conductance, and electroencephalography. These physiological measurements are becoming more commonly used within the sport psychology realm.

Perhaps it would be useful to provide an example of how a sport psychology consultant would acquire both objective and subjective measurements of arousal and anxiety to help develop an effective intervention. Let's use Joe as our example. Upon initial consultation with Joe, it would be beneficial to acquire baseline measures of how he responds to stress. Acquiring baseline information serves two purposes. First, it provides insight into how the athlete responds both physically and cognitively to stress. Secondly, it serves as a benchmark to help gauge the athlete's development throughout the training program. The initial assessment could consist of a combination of methods: interviews, questionnaires, and physiological measurements. It is dependent on the expertise of the consultant and the needs of the athlete. In Joe's case, an effective approach would be to use all three of the above-mentioned techniques. An initial assessment would consist of having Joe answer the CSAI-2 as well as asking him to provide specific examples of when he gets stressed and how it manifests itself (somatically or cognitively).

In addition to these two methods, an objective measurement using biofeedback technology would be incorporated. Joe will undergo a one-hour assessment to determine his physiological and cognitive responses to stress. This assessment is noninvasive and entails the attachment of adhesive sensors to monitor a variety of physiological and cognitive changes in an individual's body. It consists of measuring an athlete's heart rate, respiration rate, muscle tension, skin conductance, temperature, and EEG. During the assessment Joe will be asked to participate in several stressful activities (e.g., Stroop test)[1] followed by periods of relaxation. This will shed light on how Joe's mind and body respond to stressors and his ability to relax following a stressful event. Our bodies are designed to respond to stress—fight or flight response—however it is essential to be able to turn off our sympathetic nervous system once the stressor has been removed. Following the assessment, the results will be combined with the subjective measures and Joe will be provided with a report detailing his strengths and weaknesses and recommendations to improve performance. Complete Try It Out! Activity 1 on page 61 to identify how you deal with stress and anxiety.

A brief summary of Joe's hypothetical assessment will be presented to serve as a case study to help you learn how to apply the numerous anxiety-reducing techniques in the following sections. Upon amalgamating Joe's three measurements of anxiety (i.e., self-report questionnaires, interview, and objective stress test) a clearer picture emerges as to how Joe somatically and cognitively responds to stress. Physiologically, it was found that Joe has a tendency to respond to stress with an elevated heart rate, shallow rapid breaths, and increased muscle tension. Cognitively, the results revealed that Joe had a tendency to ruminate and had what is sometimes referred to as busy brain (the tendency to have excessive chatter and an inability to shut one's brain off). With regard to the objective stress test, it was found that Joe interpreted his high physiological and cognitive arousal levels as being negative and detrimental to performance. Combining all three methods ensures a complete picture of how Joe responds to stress and will guide the development of an individualized program focusing on specifically what Joe needs to work on.

Developing Interventions

*"It's not a case of getting rid of the butterflies,
it's a question of getting them to fly in formation."*

–Basketball coach Jack Donahue.

Now that you are familiar with the various methods of how to measure an athlete's arousal and anxiety levels it is time to discuss possible techniques to help tackle a variety of arousal regulation problems. It is important that athletes are aware of their own psychological states before they can learn how to control their thoughts and emotions. Once athletes are aware of their optimal arousal levels they can start to employ arousal regulation techniques.

One key thing to keep in mind when developing an intervention is the matching hypothesis. This hypothesis states that an anxiety management technique should be matched to the specific anxiety problem

---

[1] A Stroop test is a common psychological test that requires the participant to name the colour of the ink that a word is written in rather than the word itself, such as: BROWN is typed in green ink, thus the correct answer is green and an incorrect answer would be brown.

experienced by the athlete. Simply put, cognitive anxiety should be treated with mental relaxation, whereas somatic anxiety would be best matched with physical relaxation. It is important to remember that anxiety-reducing techniques are not necessarily mutually exclusive; it is possible to witness cross-over effects. That is, research has shown that the employment of a somatic anxiety relaxation technique may also produce cognitive relaxation, and cognitive techniques may reduce somatic anxiety. It is also suggested that if you are uncertain as to the type of anxiety experienced by the athlete, the best approach would be a multimodal one (i.e., cognitive and somatic techniques). The following section will discuss some possible somatic, cognitive, and multimodal techniques to reduce anxiety.

© Rena Schild, 2012. Used under license from Shutterstock, Inc.

Reducing Somatic Anxiety

How does your body respond to stress? Physiologically, when an individual is anxious, his or her heart rate increases, respiration rate is shallow and fast, palms get sweaty, temperature decreases, and muscle tension increases. Although every athlete is unique and responds to stress differently, there are two modalities—respiration rate and muscle tension—that the majority of athletes require some degree of training to learn to control. Thus, this section will focus on two somatic anxiety-reducing techniques that tackle breathing and muscle tension.

Breath Control

As noted previously, when an athlete is stressed his or her breathing is short, shallow, and irregular (see Figure 4.1). In comparison, when an athlete is calm, his or her breathing is smooth, deep, and rhythmic (see Figure 4.2). Breathing is a simple yet essential tool that can be taught to athletes. It is arguably the most indispensable somatic anxiety-reducing technique that an athlete can learn. Three reasons for its

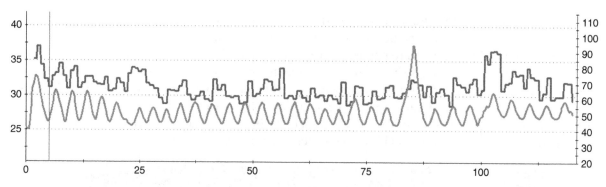

FIGURE 4.1: Respiration rate and heart rate of an anxious athlete. *Note:* top line indicates heart rate and bottom line indicates respiration rate.

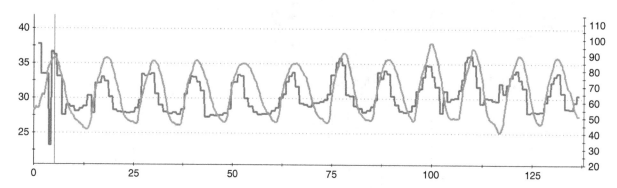

FIGURE 4.2: Respiration rate and heart rate of a calm athlete. *Note:* jagged line line indicates heart rate and rounded line indicates respiration rate.

importance are: (1) it is the link between the mind and body; (2) it brings an athlete to the here and now; and (3) it integrates the left (e.g., analytical) and right brain (e.g., emotions) functioning. Breathing is the foundation to optimal performance and lays the foundation for the acquisition of several other psychological skills.

Miller (2010) developed an excellent protocol for teaching athletes breath control. Three key components—rhythm, inspiration, and continuity—should be emphasized when teaching an athlete how to breathe. *Rhythm* refers to one's breath being slow and smooth. It is important for athletes to focus on expanding their stomachs on their inhalation. On the exhale all the air is released and the stomach should constrict. One useful tip to remember is that to engage the body and mind in relaxation, one's exhalation should be twice as long as the inhalation. For example, you can count to two on your inhale and four on your exhale. Once that becomes too easy some athletes will count to three on the inhalation and six on the exhalation. As long as the 1:2 ratio is adhered to relaxation will occur. As simple as breathing is, the majority of athletes have never been taught proper technique, and it is of value to spend time teaching athletes how to breathe properly.

© Aspen Photo, 2012. Used under license from Shutterstock, Inc.

The second component of Miller's (2010) breath control is inspiration (i.e., the in-breath). Some athletes find it useful to imagine they are drawing energy in with each breath. Miller also suggests the five-point star method where one imagines energy being transmitted to one's head, hands, and feet. The third component refers to continuity of breath. Many individuals treat breathing as two distinct acts (i.e., in and out) rather than as a continuous flow of energy. Miller uses the clever analogy of perceiving breathing as the turning of an endless wheel. You can visualize a clock and you are starting at six o'clock. Your inhale should turn the wheel up to twelve o'clock and your outbreath turns the wheel down to six o'clock.

An effective means of teaching breathing is through the use of biofeedback equipment. Typically, when athletes are hooked up for breathing training, both their respiration rate and heart rate are measured using noninvasive sensors. A respiration belt is secured around the athlete's waist and a sensor is placed on the athlete's thumb to measure heart rate. This method allows athletes to see how their body responds to stress in real time. Athletes will see on the computer screen exactly how they breathe when they are stressed versus when they are relaxed. Athletes are taught the proper way to breathe and will practice for several minutes. It is also beneficial for athletes to practice five minutes throughout their daily activities (e.g., school, car, practice, etc). Much like physical skills, the more a person practices breathing, the more the skill will become natural and automatic.

Muscle Relaxation

Muscle tension is a common physiological response to stress for athletes. This finding is not surprising considering that athletes use their muscles constantly. Muscle tension can hinder performance by reducing an athlete's accuracy and precision. An exercise highlighting this is to alternately tap your first two fingers on a table as fast as you can. You should be able to do this activity with relative ease. Now tense up your forearm and attempt to do the same exercise. You should see a noticeable decrease in your speed and dexterity. This is essentially what happens to your body when you have excessive muscle tension. Muscle tension is an issue for Joe—his passes and shots will be off target as a result.

A popular somatic anxiety-reducing technique for muscle tension is progressive relaxation. This procedure teaches you to relax your muscles through a two-step process of tensing and relaxing various muscle groups. Below is a list of the key steps involved in this technique:

- Athlete lies on back, arms to sides.
- The goal is to relax entire body in minutes.
- First you deliberately apply tension to a certain muscle group (usually start with your foot and work your way up your body).
- Then you stop the tension and turn your attention to noticing how the muscles relax as the tension flows away.
- Athlete progressively moves from one muscle group to another.
- Through repetitive practice you quickly learn to recognize—and distinguish—the associated feelings of a tensed muscle and a completely relaxed muscle.
- With this simple knowledge, you can then induce physical muscular relaxation at the first signs of the tension that accompanies anxiety.

Reducing Cognitive Anxiety

The great Yogi Berra once said, "You can't think and hit at the same time"; how right he was. This quote nicely highlights the fact that excessive thinking during athletic performances, especially at the elite level, deters from performance. Joe is an excellent example of how overthinking hinders performance. Joe finds himself overanalyzing his every movement on the ice. For instance, while on a power play he has noticed a constant inner dialogue and finds himself questioning his passing and shot selection; consequently he is making more mistakes and has been removed from the power play unit. His brain can do only one thing at a time. Joe's excessive thinking is cluttering his mind and interfering with his physical performance. Joe might learn to reduce the chatter in his mind if he reviewed the various techniques discussed to conquer cognitive anxiety.

ABCDs

This is a technique devised by Seligman (1998) and its purpose is twofold. It teaches athletes what their emotional signature is with regard to stress. Every individual responds to stressful situations differently; for example, some people respond with anger while others respond to fear or disappointment. Secondly, and perhaps most importantly, it teaches individuals to focus on what they can control and highlights their strengths and ultimately increases self-confidence.

The exercise requires athletes to write down an adversity that occurred that week. For each adversity the athletes write down their beliefs about the situation (i.e., what *thoughts* they had when it happened). Following this the athletes list the consequences of the adversity (i.e., what *feelings* they had when it happened). The final step, arguably the most important, involves the athletes providing evidence to contradict their negative thoughts and emotions. The athletes are to think like a lawyer and provide past evidence that proves they are talented. It also is beneficial to think of what they can do in the future to increase the chances they will be successful. The following is a sample of Joe's ABCDs:

ADVERSITY: I made tons of mistakes in practice today.
BELIEF (THOUGHTS): I suck. I don't deserve to be here.
CONSEQUENCES (FEELINGS): Angry and disappointed in my ability.
DISPUTATION: I had a long day and just wasn't able to focus. I am a great player and work hard. Having one bad day at practice isn't the end of the world. I'm going to work hard and start doing my pregame routine before practices to enhance my focus. I make great plays in games, and this one practice doesn't reflect my ability or define me as a hockey player. For example, last weekend against the Montreal Canadiens I had two goals and three assists and helped my team win the game. I am a great hockey player and deserve to play in the NHL.

Deep Thought

Try doing the ABCD exercise for three different adversities you faced this week. Take note of the type of thoughts and feelings you have. Most people have an emotional signature. Knowing this will help you understand yourself and what you can do to have more positive thoughts. It will also give you confidence and help you believe in yourself.

Now that you've had a chance to explore different techniques to reduce somatic and cognitive anxiety, complete Try It Out! Activity 2 on page 63 to reflect on how arousal regulation techniques can work for you.

Multimodal Techniques

This approach combines both somatic and cognitive anxiety-reducing techniques. One example is Cognitive-Affective Stress Management Training (SMT). This training teaches an athlete specific integrated coping responses using relaxation and cognitive components to control arousal. An excellent example is a technique referred to as freeze frame. This technique was developed at the Heart Math Institute. It is considered a multimodal technique because it tackles both somatic and cognitive anxiety. It employs self-talk, breath control, and imagery. It is taught most effectively using biofeedback equipment so the athlete can see the differences between their anxious states and their relaxed states. It is an excellent technique to use during games following an error. It helps athletes "let go" of a mistake by relaxing their bodies and calming their minds. The goal of freeze frame is to bring you back and allow you to refocus. Read over the steps, and then complete Try It Out! Activity 3 on page 65 to see how the freeze frame technique works for you.

Here are the steps:

1. A negative event occurs (you are upset, nervous, things went wrong).
2. Say FREEZE or STOP.
3. Do your breathing, inhale to 3 and exhale to 6.
4. Think of something positive, something that gives you confidence and continue to do your breathing.
5. If you have a problem, you can ask yourself for a solution as you do your breathing.

Summary: Putting It All Together

In this chapter we have explored the signs and symptoms associated with arousal and anxiety, various measurement tools that can be used to assess arousal and anxiety, and different strategies for regulating arousal and anxiety levels. We have also tried to emphasize the importance of the matching hypothesis for selecting the most appropriate arousal and anxiety-regulating strategies. Now it's your turn to apply all of these concepts at once. Complete the Putting It All Together activity on page 67 and design an intervention program to help Joe.

Try It Out!

Activity 1: Self-Awareness

Complete the online version of SCAT (found at www.brianmac.demon.co.uk/scat.htm) to become aware of exactly how your mind and body respond to stress. What type of anxiety did the questionnaire assess? Compare your responses to your original notes from the Deep Thought earlier; do they match up? Do you think the self-report questionnaire is a valid measure?

Activity 2: Autogenic Training

An additional anxiety-reducing technique is autogenic training. Autogenic training is a self-styled hypnosis strategy. It involves a series of exercises designed to produce two physical sensations—warmth and heaviness—and, in turn, to produce a relaxed state. Some benefits are it decreases one's heart rate, slows the respiratory system, and allows blood to flow more easily throughout the body. There are six steps: (1) induce heaviness, (2) induce warmth, (3) heart practice, (4) breathing practice, (5) abdominal practice, and (6) head practice. Here is the final formula to try out:

- I am completely calm (once).
- My right arm is very heavy (6 times).
- I am completely calm (once).
- My right arm is very warm (6 times).
- I am completely calm (once).
- My heart beats calmly and regularly (6 times).
- I am completely calm (once).
- My breathing is very calm (6 times).
- I am completely calm (once).
- My abdominal is warm (6 times).
- I am completely calm (once).
- My forehead is pleasantly cool (6 times).
- I am completely calm (once).

Did you find this exercise useful? Why or why not? Is this a somatic or cognitive anxiety-reducing technique, or is it multimodal? Justify your answer.

Activity 3: Multimodal Technique—FREEZE FRAME

Review the steps outlined in the multimodal section prior to practicing this technique. You can think of an event during the day or a problem you have, feel the emotions you did when it happened, then say "freeze," and do the breathing and subsequent steps. Try doing it in the moment when you actually get upset or nervous and/or have a problem. It takes only a minute and no one knows you are doing it. It helps bring your focus away from the negative event and negative self-talk and calms your body down. Practice makes perfect. Once you get the breathing down, it is easy. It can be used anywhere, anytime.

Figure 4.3 is an example of an athlete doing it. The heart rate is depicted by the jagged line and respiration by the rounded line. At the 25-second mark, the athlete said "freeze" and did her breathing. Notice when the athlete was upset, how out of synch her breathing and heart rate were, and how calm and in synch they were following freeze frame.

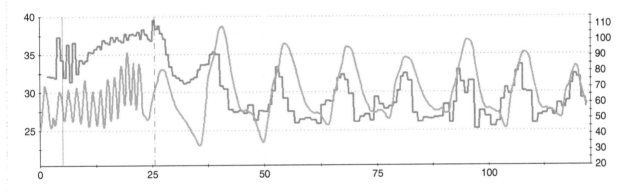

FIGURE 4.3

Putting It All Together

Now that you have learned various techniques for reducing anxiety, put on your sport psychology consultant hat and develop a program to help Joe perform optimally. Refer to his assessment results and remember to use the matching hypothesis.

Suggested Readings and References

Craft, L. L., Magyer, T. M., Becker, B. J., & Feltz, D. L. (2003). The relationship between the competitive state anxiety inventory-2 and sport performance: A meta-analysis. *Journal of Sport and Exercise Psychology, 25,* 44–65.

Crocker, P. R. E. (2007). *Sport psychology: A Canadian perspective.* Toronto, Canada: Prentice Publishing.

Davies, D. (2001). Relaxed Woods identifies the major pressure points. The Guardian, 6 April, p. 26.

Gould, D., Greenleaf, C., & Krane, V. (2002). Arousal-anxiety and sport behavior. In T. Horn (Ed.), *Advances in sport psychology* (2nd ed., pp. 207–241). Champaign, IL: Human Kinetics.

Gould, D., & Krane, V. (1992). The arousal athletic performance relationship. In T. Horn (Ed.), *Advances in sport psychology* (pp. 119–141). Champaign, IL: Human Kinetics.

Hardy, L. (1996). Testing the predictions of the cusp catastrophe model of anxiety and performance. *The Sport Psychologist,* 10, 140–156.

Hardy, L., & Parfitt, G. (1991). A catastrophe model of anxiety and performance. *British Journal of Psychology, 82,* 163–178.

Jones, G., & Swain, A. (1992). Intensity and direction as dimensions of competitive state anxiety and relationships with competitiveness. *Perceptual and Motor Skills, 74,* 467–472.

Jones, G., Swain, A. B. J., & Cale, A. (1991). Gender differences in precompetition temporal patterning and antecedents of anxiety and self confidence. *Journal of Sport and Exercise Psychology, 13,* 1–15.

Landy, F. J., & Stern, R. M. (1971). Factor analysis of a somatic perception questionnaire. *Journal of Psychosomatic Research, 15,* 179–181.

Lazarus, R. S. (1991). *Emotion and adaptation.* New York: Oxford University Press.

Martens, R. (1977). *Sport competition anxiety test.* Champaign, IL: Human Kinetics.

Martens, R., Burton. D., Vealey, R. S., Bump, L. A., & Smith, D. E. (1990). Development and validation of the Competitive State Anxiety Inventory-2. In R. Martens, R. S. Vealey & D. Burton (Eds.), *Competitive anxiety in sport* (pp. 117–190). Champaign, IL: Human Kinetics.

Maynard, I. W., Hemmings, B., & Warwick-Evans, L. (1995). The effects of a somatic intervention strategy on competitive state anxiety and performance in semi-professional soccer players. *The Sport Psychologist, 9,* 51–64.

Miller, S. L. (2010). *Performing under pressure: Gaining the mental edge in business and sport.* Mississauga, Canada: John Wiley and Sons Canada, Ltd.

Seligman, M. E. P. (1998). *Learned optimism.* New York: Pocket Books.

Smith, R. E., Smoll, F. L., & Schutz, R. W. (1990). Measurement and correlates of sport specific cognitive and somatic trait anxiety: The Sport Anxiety Scale. *Anxiety Research, 2,* 263–280.

Smith, R. E., Smoll, F. L., & Wiechman, S. A. (1998). Measurement of trait anxiety in sport. In J. Duda (Ed.), *Advances in sport and exercise psychology measurement* (pp. 105–127). Morgantown, WV: Fitness Information Technology.

Thayer, R. E. (1967). Measurement of activation through self-report. *Psychological Reports, 20,* 663–678.

Weinberg, R. S., & Gould, D. (2011). *Foundations of sport and exercise psychology* (5th ed.). Champaign, IL: Human Kinetics.

Chapter 5

Being in the Moment: Focus and Concentration

Key Concepts and Theories

- Nideffer's width and direction of attention
- Dissociation
- Internal and external distractions
- Motivation
- The choking process
- Competition routines

Choosing The Correct Focus

Owen raced home from his soccer practice and announced to his mom and dad that he "had to watch the clock." Confused they asked him to explain. Owen's coach noticed that he and the other kids were easily distracted during games and practices by things like airplanes flying overhead, blowing dandelion fluff across the field, waving to their parents on the sidelines, thinking about how tired their legs felt, worrying about their spelling test the following morning, and chatting with their friends. The coach wants the kids to practice watching a clock face, to see if they can increase their concentration ability. This is a simple exercise they can do at home where they watch the clock face and time how long their focus on the second hand of the clock can last. To do this activity focus on the second hand of the clock as it makes one complete revolution, every 5 seconds snap your fingers. On the second revolution snap your fingers every 10 seconds. Do this a third time and snap your fingers every 15 seconds (for kids who have a hard time snapping they can blink their eyes or clap their hands instead). Begin by doing this in a quiet place at home, then gradually introduce distractions to the task, like practicing in the car or with the TV on.

© Kaspri, 2012. Used under license from Shutterstock, Inc.

Owen's coach wants him and his teammates to be more focused during games and in practices. The players are distracted by *task-irrelevant cues*—things that are not related to performing well in sport at that moment. Athletes who are focused are *attending* to the correct (relevant) cues at the right time and are able to *shift* their attention as demanded by the situation. When athletes are attending to task-irrelevant cues and are distracted from focusing on what is important their performance suffers and the potential for injury increases. This chapter will examine different types of attention, consequences of attention problems, and strategies to enhance focus.

Defining Attention

Whether we use the term *focus, concentration,* or *attention,* it is a limited resource. There are limits to how much information we are able to effectively attend to at one time. As a beginner soccer player, for example, Owen must pay attention to his footwork as he dribbles the ball up the field; he would have difficulty attending to where the defenders and his teammates are located on the field. In contrast, the superstar Christiano Renaldo, dribbles the ball automatically and does not have to use his limited capacity for attention on this skill; he is able to better attend to the defenders and his teammates. Not only do we have limited capacity for attention, we must also select the *most relevant* cues to focus that limited attention on. Attending to cues that are irrelevant is the hallmark of a distracted athlete. We will further explore the consequences of a lack of attention later in this chapter.

> ### Deep Thought
>
> Select a sport skill you are familiar with. Identify the aspects of the skill that require your attention. What information or cues do not require your attention? How does your level of experience with the sport influence the cues you focus on? How might this focus change with practice in the sport?

Types of Attention

Sport generally requires four types of attention conceptualized by Nideffer: narrow internal, narrow external, broad internal, broad external. These four types include a width dimension (i.e., broad or narrow) and a direction dimension (i.e., internal or external). A narrow internal attention involves focusing inwardly (internal) on specific processes such as pacing, heart rate, breathing rate, muscle fatigue, etc. (narrow). Long distance runners, for example, likely use a narrow internal focus when deciding if they feel they have enough energy to pick up the pace late in a 10 km race. Narrow external focus is used when the athlete is focusing on one or two cues (narrow) in the environment (external). For example, a defensive player in soccer would focus on her opponent's hips to predict the direction they are going to run. This focus is external and narrow. Broad internal attention is directed inward and is used when athletes or coaches are planning such things as routines and game plans. Their attention is directed inward (internal) and is analyzing various options (broad). Broad external attention is used by athletes when they are focusing on the environment (external) and observing several relevant cues (broad). For example, a hockey player uses a broad external focus when deciding to send the puck behind the blue line. The player takes into account a number of cues (broad) occurring in the game (external) such as the score in the game, time left on the clock, where their offensive teammates are on the ice, where their defensive teammates are on the ice, etc.

Deep Thought

Select a sport you are familiar with. Describe what type of attention is required for that sport. What is the width (broad or narrow)? What is the direction (internal or external)?

Though some sports require athletes to use one type of focus more than others, most demand that athletes effectively shift their attention. An archer, for example, would primarily use a narrow external focus (the bull's eye) but would sometimes need to *shift* her attention to a broad external focus to account for range conditions such as changes in wind direction or intensity, the angle of the sun, and the like. It is often an athlete's inability to shift her attention appropriately rather than a lack of focus that will result in problems with attention. Being in the moment is critical to successful sport performance, and though it is impossible to maintain complete focus for extended periods of time, even elite performers must practice bringing their attention back to focus on the present.

Not only does the type of sport influence the width and direction of optimal attention, but the emotional and cognitive state of the athlete is also an important determinant. When athletes are anxious (see Chapter 4 for more information on anxiety) or experiencing fluctuating emotions, it is best if they focus externally on a specific task rather than internally on their anxiety or emotions (Wulf as cited in Moran, 2010). Heightened anxiety and elevated emotions can be distracting if the athlete is not able to keep them in check.

Distractions

> *"We knew she was going to be behind in the final, so the plan was to focus on her race and not worry about being behind. She stayed focused, which*

is really hard when you are a chair length behind with 50 metres to go. Her mental focus made the difference. A lot of athletes do not prepare for the unexpected and are taken by surprise."

–Peter Eriksson, coach of Chantal Petitclerc, five times gold medalist
at the 2008 Beijing Paralympic Games (Robertson, 2009).

Every day we experience things that demand our attention. We set priorities for ourselves and divide our limited resources of attention and energy to those attention-demanding activities that we deem most worthwhile. Think, for example, how often you have put off tidying your dorm room to socialize with friends instead, or when you have elected to tidy that room to put off working on a school assignment that will require significant time and effort. Some athletes and exercisers use this same technique when they purposely distract themselves from a physical activity such as long distance training runs (Morgan & Pollock, 1977) or low-intensity but sustained rowing (Tenenbaum & Connolly, 2008). This technique is called dissociation and involves thinking of task-irrelevant things, for example, watching a news program while running on the treadmill, or listening to music while weight training. Anything that directs attention away from the task and from the body is considered a dissociation strategy. In contrast, association strategies direct attention toward the body and task-relevant cues such as pacing and breathing rate. Elite athletes will use associative strategies in competitive environments or when high intensity output is demanded (e.g., marathon races [Morgan & Pollock, 1977]; high workload on a rowing ergometer [Tenenbaum & Connolly, 2008]).

Deep Thoughts:

When are some times, either in sport or every-day life, that you have used dissociation strategies? What did you do to distract yourself?

Internal distractions are anything that shifts our focus inward to task-irrelevant observations such as muscle fatigue, thinking too far into the future, dwelling on past mistakes, worrying about how others perceive us, among others. External distractions are anything that holds our outward focus to task-irrelevant cues such as fans cheering in support of the other team, poor calls by officials, repeatedly checking the scoreboard, gamesmanship or trash talking by opponents, and the like.

Some distractions are within our control; in other words, we can take steps to prevent the distractions from occurring. An example of a controllable distraction is thinking about a grumbling stomach because an athlete didn't have a snack before training. When athletes experience controllable distractions they know they could and should have prevented them by being more prepared. Distractions that are outside our control are trickier to deal with; these distractions may be unexpected or something we are unable to influence. For example, a tough tournament schedule is outside of athletes' control as they have no say in the schedule. When uncontrollable distractions occur athletes must attempt to control their reactions to the distraction. One method of doing this is to use self-talk to reframe our interpretation of the distraction (see Chapter 6 for examples). Test your understanding of internal and external distractions by completing Try It Out! Activity 1 on page 79.

Motivation can be another form of distraction. When motivation is very high athletes may try to attend to too many cues. They want to be perfect and, in a way, they "try too hard." These are athletes who attempt to do everything on the field or court and, while their effort is commendable, often they cause problems in coordinating efforts with their teammates and they spread their resources too thin. Lack of motivation can also be distracting. Thinking about how they do not want to be at practice or do not care about the outcome of a competition can interfere with performance. Jack Nicklaus, rated the best golfer of the 20th century, stated:

> *"Whenever I am up for golf—when either the tournament or course, or best of all both, excite and challenge me—I have little trouble concentrating… But whenever the occasion doesn't stimulate or challenge me, or I'm just simply jaded with golf, then is the time I have to bear down on myself with a vengeance and concentrate."*
>
> –Jack Nicklaus

Consequences of Attention Problems

When athletes get *stuck* on one type of focus and are unable to shift their attention they miss out on important cues in the environment or internally that could help them perform optimally. One of the most dramatic effects of an inability to shift attention is the phenomenon of choking. We have all seen or experienced choking in sport. Three conditions must exist for choking to potentially occur: (1) the athlete perceives the event to be important; (2) the play or moment in the competition is critical; and (3) there is opportunity for the athlete's performance to be evaluated. If an athlete is able to cope with these conditions, they will perform well; if they are unable to meet these demands, then there will be physiological changes such as increased heart rate, perspiration, and muscle tension, which leads to difficulty in coordinating body movements. In parallel the athletes' focus will become narrow and internal, and the athlete will miss cues from the environment. The result of these physiological and psychological changes is choking—a significant decrease in performance. Thinking a lot about performing actions that are usually automatic can worsen the situation and cause the athlete to perform even more poorly. Developing psychological skills, described throughout this book, can help prevent choking. Coaches can also help prevent choking by observing when the conditions for choking are developing, when athletes' physiological and/or psychological states begin to change. When these conditions begin to materialize the coach should intervene by reminding the athletes to use their psychological skills, taking a time out to talk to the athlete, or making a substitution to remove the athlete from the situation. What other methods can you think of that may be effective for preventing choking?

Deep Thought

Look up *choking* in sport on YouTube.com or a similar website, find an example of choking in sport, what factors led to the choking? Find an example of an athlete coping under pressure, what factors contributed to their success?

Another unfortunate consequence of athletes being distracted or focusing on irrelevant cues is injury. If Owen, from the opening vignette, is looking up at an airplane in the sky he is unlikely to see a gopher hole in the field and may suffer an ankle sprain as a result. This injury may have been prevented if his eyes were on the field and focused on where he was going. Other sports are riskier, and a lack of attention can have even more dire consequences. A race car driver, for example, who is distracted by internal thoughts of an argument he had with a family member or is distracted by a service engine light on the dashboard may miss a yellow caution flag signalling trouble ahead and may find himself in a collision.

© Fotokostic, 2012. Used under license from Shutterstock, Inc.

Some athletes simply focus on the wrong cues. Though less dramatic than choking, this can have an important role in how quickly an athlete acquires skills. From the opening vignette, we know Owen and his teammates spend time directing their attention to task-irrelevant cues such as dandelions and airplanes. It is likely the coach wants the team to focus on task-relevant cues such as where the ball is on the field and how the kids should contact the ball with their foot when making a pass. The next section describes techniques for helping athletes to learn to shift attention and focus on task-relevant cues.

Improving Focus Skills

Owen's soccer coach, in the opening vignette of this chapter, suggested one technique that he and his teammates can use to help develop their focus skills. Many different techniques can be used to teach and rehearse appropriate focus. Some techniques aim to maintain focus while others aim to shift focus appropriately or improve one's ability to pick out the appropriate cues. It is important that athletes who are practicing focus techniques outside of sport gradually introduce these focus skills into the sport environment, starting with training, and once they are comfortable competition settings. Complete Try It Out! Activity 2 on page 81.

Deep Thought

Observe in person or on TV athletes competing in a sport you are familiar with. Take note of the variation in pre-performance routines you observe.

Some effective methods of improving focus that are described in other chapters in this book include setting performance and process goals to focus on specific behaviours, using cue words or specific self-talk to direct attention, and using imagery to prepare for possible distractions. These psychological skills can also be used in conjunction with a pre-performance routine to produce effective focusing. Pre-performance routines involve a set sequence of behaviours that athletes repeat each time they prepare to execute a sport-specific task. For example, basketball great Reggie Miller shot 89 percent from the free-throw line using this pre-shot routine: holding the ball in his left hand he would press it against his hip while making a shooting motion with his right hand, then dribble the ball three times, and finally take his shot. Pre-performance routines are "typically composed of motor, cognitive, and emotional behaviors that are regularly performed immediately before the execution of self-paced tasks. The resulting routine is part of an athlete's repertoire when preparing to perform" (Lidor, 2010, p. 537).

Singer (1988) describes a five-step pre-performance routine for use by athletes. The components of this routine include: readying (e.g., squatting in an athletic stance at the basketball free-throw line), imaging (e.g., seeing the ball go into the net), focusing (directing attention at the ball or a spot on the backboard), executing (releasing the shot and following through), and evaluating (assessing the quality of the shot). Pre-performance routines help athletes to focus their attention on relevant cues, and this improved focus helps in performing the skill automatically so each movement does not require deliberate thought. Develop your own pre-performance routine in Try It Out! Activity 3 on page 83. Think of this routine as a final preparation for performing the task.

Summary: Putting It All Together

Focus and concentration are essential to optimal sport performance. Most athletes experience difficulty with focus at some point—focusing on the wrong things, being distracted, unable to shift focus—but can learn to improve focus and set the stage to help their concentration (e.g., by using pre-performance routines). Being focused is beneficial outside of sport as well, while driving or taking an exam, for example. To further develop your understanding of focus and concentration, complete the Putting It All Together activity in this chapter.

Try It Out!

Activity 1: Identifying Internal and External Distractions

Using your favourite sport make a list of as many internal distractions that you can think of. Next, as you did with internal distractions, make a list of as many external distractions that you can think of for your favourite sport. On your lists, mark each controllable distraction (i.e., something you may be able to control or prevent from occurring) with a "C"; mark each uncontrollable distraction (i.e., something you have no control over and will occur regardless of what you do) with a "U." Reread the vignette at the beginning of this chapter. What internal distractions were Owen and his teammates experiencing? What external distractions were they having a hard time ignoring?

Activity 2: Exercises to Improve Focus

In the space below outline a focusing activity that you could implement with athletes in a sport of your choice. What is the objective of the activity? To improve the length of time the athlete can focus? Improve selection of relevant cues? Improve ability to shift focus? Try the activity with some of your classmates. Be sure to debrief with the group following the activity and note how you could improve the activity if you were to do it again.

Activity 3: Developing a Pre-performance Routine

Choose a sport or exercise you are familiar with and is self-paced (occurs in a relatively stable setting with time for preparation). Examples of self-paced tasks are a corner kick in soccer, a serve in volleyball, and a clean-and-jerk. Using the phases for learning a pre-performance routine outlined by Lidor (2010), develop your own pre-performance routine for your selected task. Describe your experiences within each of the three phases and assess the effectiveness of your routines in each phase.

Phase 1: Preliminary Preparatory Instructions

Consider the psychological and physical preparations you already engage in prior to the task. Identify additional psychological and physical preparations that you could incorporate into your routine. Try out different combinations of preparations that are both new to you and used previously. Note which components you find useful and which are not effective.

Phase 2: Task-Specific Preparatory Instructions

Select one set of the psychological and physical routines you outlined in phase 1. This set of preparations will be your pre-performance routine. Rehearse your routine prior to performing your self-paced task in a training environment.

Phase 3: Preparatory Instructions for the Real-Life Self-Paced Event

Now that you are comfortable with your pre-performance routine practice it under conditions with two situational constraints: time constraints and external distractions. Time constraints are typically regulated under the rules of the sport. For example, in high jump athletes have one minute from when their name is called until they must perform their jump. Practice and time your pre-performance routine to ensure it fits within the rules of your sport. If your routine is too long then it needs to be adjusted. In Try It Out! Activity 1 you already identified distractions that may be present in your sport. Practice your pre-performance routine with one or two of these distractions present. Once you feel relatively comfortable with your routine under these conditions, it is time to test it in competition. Good luck!

Putting It All Together

Step 1: <u>Number Search</u>

Work in pairs with a classmate or teammate. Complete the number search below and record your score. Have your partner time you for 30 seconds, search the numbers in order starting at 01, and as you find the numbers **in order** cross them off. Your partner will do everything possible, except physically touch you, to try to distract you. Don't let him or her!

Score: _____

46	29	55	31	52	36	30	07
25	05	56	16	40	15	35	57
03	58	34	14	11	9	63	10
21	39	32	19	61	13	27	24
37	2	28	01	48	60	33	62
43	42	51	54	38	23	06	44
64	47	17	20	26	04	50	59
49	41	45	12	22	08	18	53

Step 2: <u>Identify Distractions</u>

Describe the *internal* distractions that you experienced as you completed the number search.

Describe the *external* distractions that you experienced as you completed the number search.

Step 3: <u>Refocus Plan</u>

Develop a "refocus" plan to help you concentrate when you do the activity again. Be sure to have plans for dealing with the internal and external distractions you identified above. Starting at a different number complete the number search again, using your refocusing plan.

Plan:

Score: _____

Step 4: <u>Reflecting on the Performance Plan</u>

How did your performance change? Provide an explanation for why your performance did or did not change compared to the first attempt.

What techniques did you use to cope with *internal* distractions?

What techniques did you use to cope with *external* distractions?

How motivated were you to participate in this activity? How did your level of motivation influence your performance?

What dimension of attention did you use (i.e., broad-internal, broad-external, narrow-internal, narrow-external)? Was this the most appropriate dimension to use? Explain.

Suggested Readings and References

Abernathy, B. (2001). Attention. In R. N. Singer, H. A. Hausenblas, & C. M. Janelle (Eds.), *Handbook of sport psychology* (2nd ed., pp. 53–85). New York: Wiley.

www.bleacherreport.com

Lidor, R. (2010). Pre-performance routines. In S. J. Hanrahan, & M. B. Andersen (Eds.), *Routledge handbook of applied sport psychology* (pp. 537–546). Oxon: Routledge.

Moran, A. (2010). Concentration/attention. In S. J. Hanrahan, & M. B. Andersen (Eds.), *Routledge handbook of applied sport psychology* (pp. 500–509). Oxon: Routledge.

Morgan, W. P., & Pollock, M. L. (1977). Psychological characterization of the elite distance runner. *Annals of the New York Academy of Sciences, 301,* 382–403.

www.nicklaus.com

Robertson, S. (2009). Speaking frankly: Coaches in conversation. *Coaches Plan, 16* (1), 34–35.

Singer, R. N. (1988). Strategies and metastrategies in learning and performing self-paced athletic skills. *The Sport Psychologist, 2,* 49–68.

Tenenbaum, G., & Connolly, C. T. (2008). Attention allocation under varied workload and effort perception in rowers. *Psychology of Sport and Exercise, 9,* 704–717.

Chapter 6

Self-Talk

Key Concepts and Theories

- Instructional self-talk
- Motivational self-talk
- Various self-talk strategies
- Arousal
- Focus
- Self-efficacy
- Mental toughness
- Optimism

Kayla often talks to herself while doing her swim sets. Today is no different:

Set 1: "Ughh—it feels like I am swimming in cement."
Set 2: "Shayna is already coming back? Of course she is going to lap me, I am so slow—"
Set 3: "Geez—I hate swim sets!"

This negative self-talk is not limited to practices, either. Kayla also makes negative comments about her swimming skills and abilities *during* competitions (e.g., "Oh great, you're in lane 7. You know what *that* means: 'you suck' ") as well as when she is outside of the sport (e.g., while at work: "You might as well ask for more hours, they are going to kick you off the team for being dead weight, anyway").

This season, Kayla has been underperforming relative to her own, as well as to her coaches' expectations. Her coaches have noticed this, and, during a recent individual meeting, commented that she "doesn't seem the same." They *know* she has the skills but it seems like *she* doesn't believe that she does, anymore. They concluded the meeting by informing Kayla that if her performance did not return to last-season levels by the end of the current season, she may not be invited back for next year. Kayla is very worried that she will be dropped if she can't turn things around.

It has been well-established in the sport psychology literature that what we *think* influences how we *feel*, which in turn, influences our *performance*. This performance influence can be positive or negative. This chapter focuses on the importance of understanding and being able to control one's own sport-related *thoughts*, and more specifically, one's self-talk. Controlling one's self-talk can have a substantial influence on one's feelings of confidence. Moreover, if an athlete can regulate confidence perceptions, he or she will be in a better position to achieve success—and do so *consistently*!

In this chapter we discuss how effective self-talk can influence key performance factors, such as skill and strategy learning and development, arousal levels, focus, self-efficacy, mental toughness, and optimism. Increasing one's control of these factors will subsequently increase one's confidence in his or her sport performance capabilities and, therefore, the chances of success.

Deep Thought

Use the following question to guide a discussion with your fellow classmates: Why do some people use so much negative self-talk, while others use mostly positive and/or neutral self-talk? In other words, are there factors that can influence a person's self-talk style?

Skill and Strategy Learning and Development

Whether one is learning or developing a brand-new skill or strategy, or trying to change a previously learned skill or strategy, self-talk can help. The goal of the self-talk in these situations is to gain conscious control over one's movements. Of course, the athlete's ultimate goal is to achieve automaticity with the particular skill or strategy he or she is working on (i.e., doing *without* thinking); however, until that state of automaticity is realized it is extremely beneficial to carefully construct instructional self-talk to be used during execution. It is imperative that the instructional self-talk be brief and focused on what movements the athlete needs to perform (*not* on what movements the athlete needs to avoid).

In addition, novices may benefit more from instructional self-talk that creates a mental image of what a specific body/implement position or placement *should* look like, whereas intermediates and advanced performers will benefit more from instructional self-talk that focuses on the intended movement outcome of the movement to be performed. For example, a novice swimmer might use the instructional self-talk cues "thumb the water" and "mitten," as these cues indicate that the hand should enter the water thumb-first (i.e., thumb), and that the fingers should be kept together during the pull and push phases of the stroke (i.e., mitten). Alternately, a more advanced swimmer might use the instructional self-talk cues "smooth" and "power" to metaphorically represent how the hand must enter the water (i.e., smooth) and the force that needs to be generated during the pull and push phases of the stroke (i.e., power). The specific cues used for instructional self-talk, which is oftentimes spoken to the self *during* performance execution, need to be as brief as possible to minimize the attention demands of using the self-talk, thus maximizing attention available for actual task execution.

Arousal Levels

Athletes are most likely to demonstrate *consistently* high levels of performance when they are within their optimal range for physiological and psychological activation (i.e., when they are optimally aroused). This optimal range differs from athlete to athlete, and certainly, it is advantageous for all athletes to be aware of what their optimal ranges are as well as how to assess activation levels before and during performance (see Chapter 4). Athletes can use self-talk as a tool to increase or decrease activation in order to achieve optimal arousal. Oftentimes, athletes choose to pair this form of self-talk with other psychological skills, such as imagery, relaxation, or physiological activation techniques (e.g., breath control).

Arousal regulation self-talk can vary in structure. It may comprise only a few words or it may be a sentence or more. It also may be objectively positive or negative (e.g., both "you are awesome!" and "you got nothin' left!" can be effective self-talk statements, depending on the athletes' interpretation of the statement). Of course, it can also be focused on increasing or on decreasing arousal (i.e., psyching up or calming down). The keys to effective arousal regulation self-talk is that phrases or words the athlete uses are meaningful to that particular athlete and effectively elicit the required change in his or her activation level *without* increasing anxiety levels. For example, a football player who needs to psych up after a long bus ride to an opponent's stadium may take a moment in the locker room to say to himself: "Come on, now! Big game! Get ready, be ready! Let's go!" These phrases may cause an increase in arousal, and ideally, place the athlete within his optimal range for physiological and psychological activation. An important benefit of educating athletes on effective self-talk is that the chance of *over-arousal* through the use of self-talk statements is reduced; it is important to convey to athletes that the goal of any arousal regulation self-talk is to get them into their optimal arousal zone, which is where they need to be if they aspire to *consistently* achieve optimal performance.

Focus

Self-talk can also assist athletes in controlling their attention, and more specifically, helping them to control *what* they are paying attention to, at any given point in time. A common error committed by coaches and athletes alike is thinking that as long as athletes are thinking about their sport, and not about some other aspect of their life outside of sport (e.g., school, relationships, work, etc.), they are "focused." This is incorrect. A focused athlete is an athlete who is focused on the *present*—on what he or she is doing at that *precise* moment in time—not just generally focused on the sport. For example, a water polo athlete is *unfocused* when her thoughts wander to "I would have …" thoughts (e.g., "If I had only gotten my hands up on that last play, *I would have* blocked that pass") or to "I will …" thoughts (e.g., "If I play really well today *I will* get to travel to the Hawaii tournament"). These types of thoughts do not positively affect current performance and may actually have a negative performance effect if they lead to increased anxiety or misdirected focus. Using self-talk to focus (or refocus) on the "right now" will help position the athlete for successful performance execution (e.g., hands up, get between ball and net, etc.).

Self-Efficacy, Mental Toughness, and Optimism

What we say to ourselves about our own skills and abilities typically has a greater impact on our perceptions than what anyone else says about our skills and abilities. If athletes do not *believe* they can be successful it will not matter what others say to try to convince them otherwise. Moreover, if the athletes *are* successful despite doubting their skills and abilities, they will likely attribute that success to luck or some other external factor, rather than to their own actions.

> ### Deep Thought
>
> What theories from your sport psychology course might help to explain why it's important that we believe in our skills and abilities as they pertain to a specific task or behaviour? Go beyond simply naming the theory—using a specific sport situation, explain how you think the theory (or theories) can help us understand the relationship between self-efficacy and performance.

Within a given competition or performance, the number of sport-related tasks for which an athlete has high self-efficacy beliefs will influence how mentally tough that athlete will be in challenging situations and how optimistic the athlete will be about the likelihood of success in that situation. The more mentally tough and optimistic an athlete is in a given competition, the greater the chances for successful performance. This is not to say that having high self-efficacy beliefs for only a few sport-related tasks for a given competition or performance is inconsequential; certainly, research has shown that more self-efficacious athletes outperform those with lower self-efficacy beliefs. However, it makes sense that the more tasks for which a person has high self-efficacy beliefs, the more likely he or she will be to persevere through tough situations (i.e., mental toughness) as well as the more likely the person will be to anticipate a successful performance (i.e., optimism). Thus, using a strategy such as self-talk to increase self-efficacy for various tasks can greatly benefit any athlete.

Self-talk intended to increase self-efficacy should be composed of positive statements that convey that the athlete is capable of success at the task at hand. Again, the specific words or phrases used should be personalized for the athlete so that they are meaningful, and thus, more effective. In addition, it is important to note that efficacy beliefs can be transient; therefore, the use of self-efficacy-building self-talk needs to be employed *consistently* before, during, and perhaps, even after a performance. For example, following a subjectively unsuccessful performance, the use of positive self-efficacy-building self-talk statements can help to minimize the potential damage to one's self-efficacy perceptions that can result following poor performance execution or even objective failure.

> ## Deep Thought
>
> Discuss with your fellow classmates how self-talk statements may differ depending on whether the self-talk is used before, during, or after performance. Consider things like the content of the self-talk, the intended goal of the self-talk (i.e., what it is supposed to "do" for the athlete), and the structure of the self-talk (e.g., words, tone, statement length, and any other characteristics you might think of).

Complete the Try It Out! Activity 1 on page 95 to get an idea of the self-talk you use when you are subjectively *unsuccessful* as well as when you are subjectively *successful* in sport. You will also get a chance to identify when you tend to make these self-talk statements, as well as an opportunity to observe possible relationships between your self-talk and your subsequent behaviours.

Self-Talk Strategies

It is important for an athlete to not only become aware of the self-talk that he or she uses in different situations, but he or she must also decide whether that self-talk is helping or hurting performance. If an athlete's self-talk is hurting performance via negative effects on the athlete's sport-relevant affect, cognitions, or behaviours, then it is advisable that the athlete work to revise, and ultimately, to control his or her thoughts in those particular situations where self-talk is negatively influencing performance. Remember, what an athlete says to him- or herself (i.e., what he or she believes regarding sport-relevant abilities and skills) can have a substantial influence on sport cognitions, affect, and behaviours.

Notice that we imply in the previous paragraph that self-talk is not a psychological skill that is to be used all of the time. Imagine if you were constantly speaking to yourself during practice or competition. It would be completely overwhelming as it would use up most all of your attentional resources. You simply would not be able to devote an adequate amount of focus to anything except structuring your self-talk. Clearly, that is not an effective use of this psychological skill. *Effective* self-talk use, on the other hand, requires an athlete to *selectively* and *consciously* apply self-talk in performance situations where that athlete is consistently lacking self-efficacy, finds him- or herself consistently outside of his or her optimal arousal level, or is consistently unfocused or misfocused.

Complete Try It Out! Activity 2 on page 97 to evaluate your self-talk and to gain some insight into what types of things you say that might be hurting your performance as well as the self-talk that may be 'helping' your performance. In increasing your awareness of the effects of your self-talk, you will be better prepared to regulate any self-talk you have identified as having a negative effect on your performance.

Summary: Putting It All Together

You now can probably see why self-talk is considered a psychological *skill*: after all, an athlete must learn to use it effectively, just as he or she would a physical skill. To effectively use self-talk, an athlete must first identify the performance situations where consciously controlled self-talk might be helpful, and then, *consistently* employ a self-talk strategy in an effort to eradicate the negative cognitions that are impairing performance. To check your understanding of self-talk concepts, design a self-talk intervention for yourself in the Putting It All Together activity in this chapter.

Try It Out!

Activity 1: What Are You Saying to Yourself, About Yourself?

Recall a particularly memorable sport competition you were in where you *performed poorly* and *failed* (based on your own definitions of "poor performance" and "failure"). Take a few minutes and try to mentally recreate several specific performance situations from that competition, in which you felt great pressure to do well (but were unsuccessful). Use your imagination and create a mental movie of these specific performance situations: concentrate on accurately and vividly recreating what you did, saw, heard, felt, thought, and said (to yourself), in each unsuccessful situation. This should be an effortful activity. Mentally recreating an event from the past is challenging and requires great focus and concentration. Expect that it may take you a few minutes to get your "mental movie" going in your mind.

As things that you thought or said to yourself come into your mind, write them down in the far left column below. Stick to recording the consistent and meaningful thoughts and self-talk that you recall—the ones that you think influenced your performance in some way. Once you have written down all that you can remember thinking and saying to yourself in those various unsuccessful situations, complete columns 2 and 3 for each self-talk statement you've identified.

Next, do the same thing again, but this time, recall a particularly memorable sport competition in which you *performed well* and were *successful*.

We've provided a few examples to help guide you. Use an additional piece of paper if needed.

Self-Talk Content: What did you say to yourself? Record both "good" and "bad" self-talk.	When exactly did you say it: before, during, or after actual performance execution? (Be as specific as you can.)	Outcome of subsequent performance? (e.g., the specific skill, strategy, or responsibilities you were to be executing at that point in time).
That break in the green is huge! I'll never make this putt.	Before, while I was lining up a golf putt.	I missed the putt.
It feels like I'm not even trying!	After making a bunch of jump-shots in a row during a basketball game.	I was on fire for the rest of that quarter.

Activity 2: What Types of Self-Talk Are You Using?

Go through your Try It Out! Activity 1 list. For each of the self-talk statements that you recalled for Activity 1 (i.e., thoughts and statements) identify whether the thought or statement was:

1. Positive, negative, or neutral (it would be neutral if it did not make you feel 'better' or 'worse' about yourself, such as when using instructional self-talk or self-talk to direct your focus), and
2. 'Helpful' or 'hurtful' to your learning or performance of a skill or strategy, to your focus, your arousal level, or your self-efficacy for a specific sport task. It's possible for a single self-talk statement to influence two or more of these things.

Create two separate lists: One for the self-talk you used for your subjective *failure* identified in Activity 1, and the other list for the self-talk that accompanied the *successful* situation from Activity 1.

Once these two lists are completed, identify and briefly discuss any differences you see between the types of things you say to yourself when you are unsuccessful versus successful. Are you able to detect any patterns? Why do you think you demonstrate these self-talk tendencies?

This activity, when paired with self-awareness of your self-talk during competition, can help you identify when you may be negatively influencing your own performance by using ineffective self-talk.

Putting It All Together

Design Your Own Self-Talk Intervention

An athlete can choose to implement any of several different self-talk strategies. These can vary from simple, structured self-talk statements, such as when designing the exact words or phrases one will use when performing a relatively new skill (i.e., instructional self-talk), to much more elaborate, but more loosely structured, self-talk strategies that involve using self-talk to discredit a specific thought that enters one's conscious mind and then re-focusing on the task at hand using additional self-talk. Your course textbook and/or your instructor's self-talk lecture should cover at least a few of these strategies.

In this activity, you will be creating your own self-talk intervention for *one* specific performance situation wherein you consistently experience negative self-talk. Completing this activity should give you some insight into how much thought and consistent cognitive effort must go into effective self-talk use.

Complete the following items:

1. Identify a specific performance situation wherein you *consistently* use negative or debilitating self-talk. Note that "consistent" is not the same as "frequent"; by "consistent" we mean negative self-talk statements you make *virtually every time* you are in that specific situation. With regard to specificity, you can, for example, speak to the learning of a specific skill or strategy, facing a particular opponent, being in a particular competition, striving for a specific performance goal, and so on.
2. List the types of things you *consistently* say to yourself in these situations (i.e., your negative self-talk) that hurts your performance.
3. If needed, use your sport psychology textbook (rather than this supplemental manual) or lecture notes to review the different self-talk strategies that athletes can choose to use when designing a self-talk program (e.g., thought-stopping, countering, reframing, etc.). From all of the self-talk strategies you could use, select the specific self-talk strategy that you think is *most appropriate* for the situation you identified in item 1. What self-talk strategy did you choose? Briefly overview it, in your own words.
4. Discuss *why* you think this specific strategy is most appropriate for you and your negative self-talk situation you identified.

5. Using the specific self-talk strategy you selected in item 3, create the self-talk statements that you will use to help improve your performance in the specific situation you identified in item 1. Remember to consider the negative self-talk that you are currently using in that situation when deciding how you will structure your self-talk intervention. Some self-talk strategies are more appropriate than others, depending on the nature of the negative self-talk that you are trying to eliminate. For this item (item 5), identify:

   a. What your self-talk statement(s) are.
   b. Where you will use them (practice, competition, training, outside of sport, rehabilitation, etc.).
   c. When you will use them (before, during, and/or after performance, only when negative self-talk arises, on a regular schedule, etc.).
   d. Why you think this *specific* self-talk intervention you have designed will improve your performance in the *specific* situation you are addressing (i.e., how will using this self-talk intervention change your performance?).

Suggested Readings and References

Bandura, A. (1997). *Self-efficacy: The exercise of control*. New York: Freeman.

Crocker, P. R. E. (2011). *Sport and exercise psychology: A Canadian perspective* (2nd ed.). Toronto, Canada: Pearson.

Hardy, J., Gammage, K., & Hall, C. (2001). A descriptive study of athlete self-talk. *The Sport Psychologist*, 15, 306–318.

Weinberg, R. S., & Gould, D. (2007). *Foundations of sport and exercise psychology* (4th ed.), Champaign, IL: Human Kinetics.

Williams. J. M. (2010). *Applied sport psychology: Personal growth to peak performance* (6th ed.). New York, NY: McGraw-Hill.

Chapter 7

Optimizing Imagery Use

Key Concepts and Theories

- Lang's bioinformational theory
- Internal and external imagery perspectives
- Paivio's 5 functions of imagery: cognitive specific, cognitive general, motivational specific, motivational general-arousal, motivational general-mastery
- Modeling
- Goal setting
- Self-talk

Taking the Next Step

Kayla: "Hi coach. I know you've taken some coaching courses lately and I'm wondering if you know anything about the mental game. I watched an interview of Tiger Woods and he says his mental game is really important. Do you think that's something I could do and that would help me step up my swimming to the next level?"

Coach: "Sure Kayla, from what I've learned all athletes can benefit from upping their mental game. There are some things I've learned from my coaching courses; maybe they can help you too. If it's okay with you I'd like to do this with the whole swim team as I think everyone could benefit from it."

K: "That would be awesome."

C: "Okay, great. I'll also talk to the sport psychology professor at the university to get her advice, too. Maybe she has a graduate student who would be willing to help us out."

K: "Sounds good to me."

C: "Is there anything in particular about the mental side of swimming that you'd like to focus on?"

K: "I'm not sure exactly. But, confidence seems to be a big thing. I've noticed I swim well at races when I feel confident. So, something to help me feel confident more often would be fantastic."

C: "Hmmm—one strategy I'm thinking of is imagery. It's a mental skill we learned about in our coaching courses and they said it can help with lots of things like confidence, reaching goals, learning skills, and staying motivated. It's also a technique I used often when I was on the national swim team. I'll look back over my notes, talk to the prof, and then set something up with the team."

K: "Sweet, thanks coach. See you at the pool later."

C: "Will do Kayla."

Kayla wants to gain a competitive edge over her competition and get closer to her goals by incorporating sport psychology into her regime. Her swim coach highlighted some of the purposes that athletes use imagery for (see Martin, Moritz, & Hall, 1999). Coach also mentioned that national team athletes often use imagery; higher level athletes are more likely to employ imagery than athletes of lower competitive levels. In this chapter we will explore how to use imagery effectively, how imagery ability can be improved, and how to incorporate imagery into sport and exercise settings.

Defining Mental Imagery

Mental imagery is often called *visualization*, though these are poor synonyms. Imagery incorporates more than the visual sense and effective imagery uses multiple senses. To experience imagery do the first Try It Out! activity in this chapter.

Deep Thoughts

Based on what you have read about imagery and your experience with the Try It Out! activity, how would you define imagery?
Assume you are teaching a group of youth athletes to use imagery. First you start with a definition of imagery. In your own words, what would you tell them?

You have likely already explored different theories that help to explain why imagery is effective. We can illustrate some of those theories through practical activities. One theory is Lang's bioinformational theory. Lang's theory focuses on emotion-laden response propositions. Choose a sport or physical activity you are familiar with. Write an emotion-focused imagery script and measure your heart rate (wear a heart rate monitor or use biofeedback if available or take your heart rate before and after). Try re-creating positive and negative emotions. Which is more salient? What happens to your heart rate in relation to the images you experience?

Imagery can also be viewed as sending low-level impulses or signals from the brain to activate the same pattern in the muscles as though the athlete or exerciser were actually performing the action. Check out this video online (http://www.youtube.com/watch?v=vD06AfbmFlY) to see imagery in action. Do the following activity to experience imagery yourself: Use a string with nut on the end (you may also use a key or something similarly weighted) as in the photo below. Rest your elbow on the table in front of you, hold the string between your thumb and forefinger, allowing the nut to dangle at the end of the string (see the photo below). Have someone else observe you as you do the activity. After reading the directions close your eyes, take a deep, slow breath in, slowly exhale, and set aside any extraneous thoughts for now. Picture in your mind the string with the nut on the end. Feel the weight of the string and nut in your hand. Now imagine the nut moving from side to side, across your body. Notice the feel of the pendulum movement. Now see the string and nut change direction; imagine it moving toward you and away from you. Notice the smooth rhythm and movement. See if you can speed up your image; then see it slowing down. As the image of the string and nut slows, see them change direction again; this time the string and nut move in a circle. Try to imagine a wide circle; picture it. Then imagine the circle getting faster and tighter; eventually the nut stops. Open your eyes. Ask the observer what he or she saw. Did the string and nut move in the direction as suggested by the imagery script? Were you able to create an image of the string and nut? Were you able to vividly imagine the changes in the movement of the nut and string?

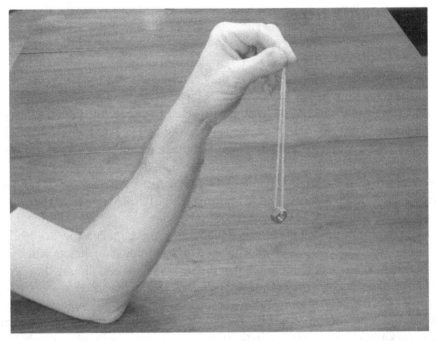

Courtesy of Melanie Gregg

Imagery Ability

Our ability to form images and the effectiveness of those images are influenced by the visual quality of the images, clarity, vividness, ability to manipulate or control the images, experiencing multiple senses (i.e., smell, sound, etc.) while imaging, and many other factors. Athletes who are able to see themselves transition from swimming in a training environment to the national championships are demonstrating manipulation of the image. Some athletes have difficulty completing an image; for example, an athlete could see herself going over only the first few hurdles in a 100m hurdle race (there are 10 hurdles in the race) and was never able to see herself completing the race. This indicates that maintaining an image was difficult for this athlete. A golfer who imagines the weight of the club in his hand, the kinaesthetic or physical feeling of the swing of the golf club, the sound of the club contacting the ball, the smell of freshly mowed grass, and the sound of the wind rustling the trees, senses creating a more vivid imagery experience. Athletes who are better at imagery report using imagery often and athletes who use imagery frequently indicate their imagery is effective compared to athletes who struggle to create, maintain, or experience images.

Another aspect of imagery is perspective. This refers to the viewpoint of the person using imagery. An internal imagery perspective is from within, as though you are looking from your own eyes. For example, a soccer player might image the ball rolling across the grass toward her feet, see where her teammates and opponents are on the field, feel her leg swing back and then forward, making contact with the ball, hear the thud of her foot against the ball, and feel her leg follow through after contacting the ball. She would not see what is happening behind her, or outside her field of vision, and she would not see the play from above. Athletes using an external perspective view themselves as though they are watching a video recording. For example, a gymnast may see himself on the rings, he may view his movements from the perspective of where the judges are located, being sure he is technically proficient. Most athletes will naturally find one perspective easier to use. Athletes in interactive sports (e.g., soccer, basketball, racquetball) generally find that an internal perspective provides them with more information, so they can imagine themselves in relation to other players or an object such as a ball. Athletes in form-based sports (e.g., figure skating, diving, Olympic weightlifting) generally find that an external perspective provides them with more information; they can image their body in relation to the space around them and assess their form from various angles. Most athletes find one perspective more natural and will often shift from one perspective to another. It is best to encourage athletes to try using both perspectives. Think back to your experience of images A and B in Try It Out! Activity 1: did you have a preferred imagery perspective? Consider why you may have selected one perspective over the other.

You may already be aware of some methods of assessing imagery ability. The most common means is by self-report questionnaires (e.g., MIQ-R, Hall & Martin, 1997; MIAMS, Gregg & Hall, 2006b; VMIQ-2, Roberts, Callow, Hardy, Markland, & Bringer, 2008). There are also some brain-imaging techniques that have outlined areas of the brain that are engaged while imaging (e.g., D'Esposito, 1997). Assessing imagery ability is useful for imagery researchers who need to determine if an athlete will benefit from an imagery-training program (some people report an inability to form images, though they are likely to be able to form at least part of an image). The assessment categorizes athletes based on their imagery ability, and can determine the effectiveness of an imagery intervention by assessing imagery ability before and after the intervention. Sport psychology consultants may also find it useful to assess the imagery ability of the athletes they work with to give them an indication of the starting point of each athlete, how much time they should devote to developing the athletes' imagery ability, and how effective the imagery is for the desired outcomes (e.g., enhanced sport confidence, decreased anxiety, greater focus). Complete the second Try It Out! activity in this chapter to assess your imagery ability.

Deep Thoughts

Choose a familiar sport skill. Imagine the skill from your natural perspective (internal or external). Imagine the skill again, but from the other perspective. Which perspective provided you with more information for that sport? Which perspective did you find easier to use? Could you incorporate multiple senses into your image—visual, kinaesthetic, audible, and smell?

Seeing Imagery in Practice

In the opening vignette of this chapter the swim coach planned to contact a sport psychology consultant to help the team learn to use imagery. Because Kayla was concerned specifically about confidence the consultant decided to focus on motivational-general mastery imagery. You have probably read about the five functions of imagery use in sport identified by Hall and his colleagues. It is important to match the function of imagery used to the intended outcome. For example, since Kayla wants to increase her sport confidence then motivational-general mastery imagery should be used. This function of imagery focuses on images that contain challenges that the athlete successfully overcomes, and is the most common reason athletes give for using imagery. Kayla may imagine herself behind the leaders at the halfway point of a swim race. She sees herself relax her shoulders so her stroke becomes smoother. This allows her pace to quicken and she reels in the leaders as the race progresses. In this image Kayla may also include other functions of imagery such as feeling her smooth strokes (cognitive specific—images of sport skills); being congratulated by her parents after her race (motivational specific—images of rewards or goal achievement); executing her race plan (cognitive general—images of race plans, routines, game plays); seeing herself controlling her emotions and staying calm on the starting block (motivational general-arousal—images of arousal and emotion regulation).

Deep Thoughts

Consider your experiences in sport, what are some images you have used in the past? When were you likely to use imagery?

© Sergey Peterman, 2012. Used under license from Shutterstock, Inc.

Imagery can be used whenever athletes can make time for it and wherever they find it useful. Most athletes find it most effective to use imagery just before and during competition. Some functions of imagery, such as cognitive specific and cognitive general, may be most useful during training when athletes are trying to learn or refine sport skills and tactics. Coaches can easily encourage their athletes to use imagery during training. For example, if Kayla was working on her flip turn technique before each turn the coach could instruct her to imagine executing a perfect turn. After each turn that goes well Kayla should also imagine that turn so she can ingrain the technique into her muscle memory. Imagery should first be rehearsed in training before athletes implement it in competition settings.

Imagery is commonly used in conjunction with other psychological skills. We have already discussed that motivational-specific imagery is related to goal setting. Motivational general-arousal imagery is an arousal-regulation technique. Self-talk is frequently a companion to imagery. Imagery of being focused and selecting the correct cues in the sport environment helps athletes focus their attention. Imagery can be used in conjunction with most other sport psychology techniques. Most notably, imagery has strong ties to the technique of modeling (see Chapter 8).

Summary: Putting It All Together

Imagery is a commonly used sport psychology technique; its effectiveness can be enhanced through regular practice. Athletes who practice imagery will also become better at imagery and this will further have a positive effect on performance. The activities in this chapter were designed to increase your understanding of imagery, your awareness of your own imagery ability, and your ability to use tools to help you practice and improve your imagery experiences. To further your understanding of imagery, complete the Putting It All Together activity at the end of this chapter.

Try It Out!

Activity 1: Experiencing Imagery

Read the sample imagery scripts below, try to image them, then rate your experience of each image.

Image A

Imagine you are playing a game of soccer. You see yourself standing on the field in a ready position. You see your teammate kick the ball toward you and you imagine the ball flying through the air toward you. You see it land just in front of you on the field, see your foot make contact with the ball, and see the ball travel toward the goal. The keeper lunges for the ball and just manages to get fingertips on it, preventing a goal.

Use a scale of 1 (difficult to see/feel) to 7 (very easy to see/feel) to rate your image of the scene. How difficult or easy was it to see the ball travelling toward you? Did you see your teammates on the field? How difficult or easy was it to feel your foot contact the ball? How intensely did you experience emotion when the keeper stopped the goal? What other senses were you able to incorporate into your image of the scenario?

Image B

Imagine you are playing a game of soccer. You see yourself standing on the field in a ready position. You feel your quadriceps flex, ready for movement. The grass was mowed just before the game and the smell of fresh cut grass stings your nose. The breeze is making your jersey flutter slightly. The whistle blows; you see your teammate kick the ball and imagine the ball flying through the air toward you. You see it land just in front of you on the field with a soft thud, feel your foot make contact with the ball, and see the ball travel toward the goal. As you hold your breath, the keeper lunges for the ball and just manages to get fingertips on it, preventing a goal.

Use a scale of 1 (difficult to see/feel) to 7 (very easy to see/feel) to rate your image of the scene. How did the image of this scene compare to your image of scene A? Was one more vivid than the other? Did you find it more difficult to experience some senses compared to others? What role do you think experience with the sport may play in your experience of the image?

Activity 2: Assessing Imagery Ability

In the reference list to this chapter there is a list of imagery ability measures. Choose one, complete the questionnaire, score it, and reflect on if you would benefit from improving your imagery ability. Are you better able to experience kinaesthetic or visual images? Do you find it easier to image from an external or internal perspective?

Putting It All Together Activity

Tennis Ball Activity

Students will complete the task individually. This is a hand–eye coordination task that requires bouncing (at least one bounce) tennis balls into a bin without banking them off the wall. You will stand 3 metres from the bin and will have 20 seconds to complete the task.

Trial 1 score: Trial 2 score:

Reflection Task

Pre-Trial 2

1. Complete an imagery ability measure.

2. Write down an imagery script that you will follow prior to performing the task for trial 2. Try to be as descriptive as you can and include multiple senses.

Post -Activity

Do you believe the imagery helped or hindered your performance? Why?

How vivid was your imagery? Do you think that you are good at imagery? How does this relate to your score on the imagery ability measure?

What perspective (internal or external) did you use in your images? Which imagery perspective would be most appropriate for this task, given what we know about perspective?

What function(s) of imagery did you use (i.e., CG, CS, MG-M, MG-A, MS)? Provide specific examples. Explain why you chose to use those functions. How does this fit with Martin et al.'s applied model of imagery use in sport?

Suggested Readings and References

D'Esposito, M., Detre, J. A., Aguirre, G. K., Stallcup, M., Alsop, D. C., Tippet, L. J., & Farah, M. J. (1997). A functional MRI study of mental image generation. *Neuropsychologia, 35,* 725–730.

Gregg, M., & Hall, C. (2006a). The relationship of skill level and age to the use of imagery by golfers. *Journal of Applied Sport Psychology, 18,* 363–375.

Gregg, M., & Hall, C. (2006b). Measurement of motivational imagery abilities in sport. *Journal of Sports Sciences, 24,* 961–971.

Hall, C. R., & Martin, K. A. (1997). Measuring movement imagery abilities: A revision of the movement imagery questionnaire. *Journal of Mental Imagery, 21,* 143–154.

Martin, K. A., Moritz, S. E., & Hall, C. R. (1999). Imagery use in sport: A literature review and applied model. *The Sport Psychologist, 13,* 245–268.

Roberts, R., Callow, N., Hardy, L., Markland, D., & Bringer, J. (2008). Movement imagery ability: Development and assessment of a revised version of the Vividness of Movement Imagery Questionnaire. *Journal of Sport and Exercise Psychology, 30,* 200–221.

Weinberg, R., Butt, J., Knight, B., Burke, K. L., & Jackson, A. (2003). The relationship between the use and effectiveness of imagery: An exploratory investigation. *Journal of Applied Sport Psychology, 15,* 26–40.

Chapter 8

Modeling

Key Concepts and Theories

- Social learning theory
- Self-efficacy theory
- Functions of observational learning

Introduction to Modeling

Modeling (sometimes referred to as observational learning, vicarious learning, or role modeling) is a psychological technique often found in motor learning texts but not in sport psychology texts. In fact, you may be more familiar with this technique from your motor learning and motor control courses than your sport and exercise psychology courses. This may be a new topic in your course, or perhaps your instructor included this within a section on sport psychology intervention techniques. The notion of learning from viewing a demonstration, reviewing videotape of ourselves to improve performance, or creating highlight tapes as a form of precompetition preparation is certainly a technique applied in coaching and in sport settings. In this chapter we'll explore how you may use modeling within sport and exercise settings.

Deep Thought

Think of the last time you were preparing for a sporting event. Who did you watch in practice? Before, during, or after you competed? Compare and contrast how you used observation in these settings. Did you watch other athletes? Coaches? Opponents? Yourself? Why did you watch those people? Consider situations both where your coach or trainer asks you to watch a demonstration, as well as situations in which you decided to watch others (or yourself) for some reason.

Applied Model for the Use of Observation

There are many reasons why athletes and coaches may choose to observe others; perhaps it is to work on specific skills and strategies, to compare themselves to someone else as a way of boosting confidence or forming beliefs about their capabilities, or maybe it is to see how others deal with a challenging situation (e.g., competitive stressors) and learn how to cope themselves. Athlete and coaches may also choose to videotape themselves and watch it as a way of improving their performance as well. Once you decide to use modeling as a technique, you may have lots of questions. Who should I watch? What should I pay attention to? Does the angle or speed of the demonstration matter? Given the large number of factors to consider, we can use Ste-Marie et al.'s (2012) recently proposed Applied Model for the Use of Observation as a way to help organize our thoughts and plan how we might structure a modeling experience.

Below is a diagram showing the components of the model and how they interact. The idea is that if we know what the moderator variables look like (i.e., the learner and the situation) and we know the desired outcome (goal), we can then identify the proper context and function and design the intervention characteristics accordingly. As you read through each of the following sections of this chapter, work your way through Try It Out! Activity 1 on page 123 to help you plan an observational learning intervention. When you are done, you will see how you can apply research to create an evidence-based intervention.

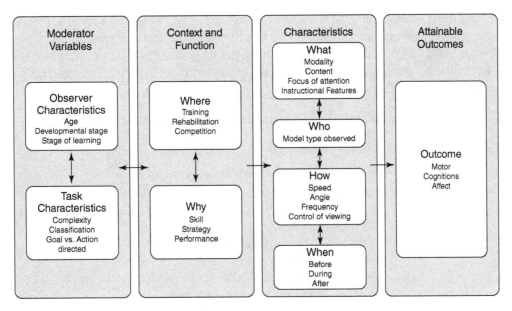

"Observation Interventions for Motor Skill Learning and Performance: An Applied Model for the Use of Observation" by Diane M. Ste-Marie, Barbi Law, Amanda M. Rymal et al. *International Review of Sport and Exercise Psychology*, March 2012, Taylor and Francis. Reprinted by permission of the publisher (Taylor & Francis Ltd., http://www.tandf.co.uk/journals).

When and Where to use Modeling

Let's return to Kayla and her goal of improving her personal best swim time. She has heard that modeling is one way to enhance her performance, but when and where should she begin?

Modeling can be used in various movement contexts: practice, competition, injury rehabilitation, and exercise or physical training. Depending on whether you are reviewing video or watching a live model, there is also the possibility that you can use modeling before, during, or after you physically complete skills in any of these situations. When do you think it would be most beneficial for Kayla to observe her swim performance? When would modeling be most helpful for building her confidence?

Why to Use Modeling

When we refer to the function of observational learning or modeling, we are referring to *why* any learner would use modeling. The function is directly linked to the desired outcome. For example, Kayla coaches young swimmers. She has a student, Emma, in her class who is scared of the deep end of the pool. Emma is not confident in her swimming abilities and, when she was younger, fell off the dock at her cottage into deep water and panicked. As a coach, Kayla might choose to use modeling with Emma to help her overcome her fear and anxiety and to help build her confidence. This would reflect the performance function. Kayla may watch other swimmers at meets to see how they handle the stress of competing. This would also be an example of the performance function.

However, when Kayla is at practice, she might choose to observe other swimmers or watch video of her own swimming in order to plan her race strategy (i.e., the strategy function) or to work on elements of her technique (i.e., the skill function). All three of these functions can be used within practice and competition settings. Kayla could also use more than one function at a time. For example, she may observe video of herself from her last swim meet in order to critique her technique (i.e., the skill function) and to build her confidence that her new technique is paying off and helping her to swim faster and faster with each race (i.e., the performance function).

Deep Thought

Not only do athletes use modeling, but coaches and sport officials also use modeling to help them learn skills and strategies, and to regulate their mental state to enhance performance. Drawing on your own experiences, or by watching footage of a sporting event, develop an example for a sport situation when a coach or official may use modeling for each of the three functions. Since this is an area where there hasn't been a lot of research to date, it is possible there are other functions that modeling may serve for these two roles in sport. Are there other reasons for which they may use modeling? Form a group of three or four students and discuss your ideas.

Who to Observe

Now that you have identified the moderating variables (i.e., the athlete and task characteristics), as well as the desired outcome, the sporting context, and functions, it is time to consider who the ideal model for Kayla may be.

Part of the decision for whom to have as the "model" relies on practicality—is it possible to video the athlete and edit it to show what you would like? Do you have access to footage of an elite athlete doing the same skill or facing the same challenges? Is there another athlete in the same training group who can provide a demonstration? Ultimately, your goal is to find a model who is close to what would be optimal for achieving your desired outcomes. What is the ideal model? There are several model characteristics to consider.

First and foremost, the model should be someone that the observer can relate to in some way. Think back to your class notes on social learning theory (Bandura, 1986) and self-efficacy theory (Bandura, 1997). Both of these theories discuss the idea that vicarious experiences (i.e., modeling) are more effective when there is a high degree of model–observer similarity. This similarity could be in terms of skill level, but it could also be in terms of other factors such as age and gender. Consider the examples of Kayla and Emma. What model characteristics do you think would be important for them to be able to relate to the model? Complete Try It Out! Activity 2 on page 125 to help you identify key model characteristics for both Kayla and Emma.

In addition to model–observer similarity, there are other model characteristics to consider, such as physical skill level and psychological states. A model's physical skills are usually defined as high (i.e., expert), intermediate, and low (i.e., learning) based on how closely they can approximate the "perfect" or "correct" behaviour. We can combine skill level with psychological states, or beliefs about performance, to create models that exhibit both high skill level and positive beliefs about their abilities (i.e., mastery models) as well as those that are still developing their physical skills and progressively show more positive beliefs about their abilities (i.e., coping models). From which of these model types do you think Emma would benefit the most?

After reading about model–observer similarity and different skill levels, you may have thought to yourself, "Wouldn't seeing myself be the ideal in terms of similarity?" and "I wonder how easy it is to edit mistakes out of a video." With the availability of video cameras and editing programs such as iDVD and MovieMaker, it is rather easy to create a modeling video of yourself. This type of modeling is called "self-as-a-model" and can be simple video replay, or edited to show only correct performances. A special type of self-modeling, called feedforward self-modeling, involves editing the video to show athletes completing a skill perfectly that they have never done without errors or showing them completing the skill in a new context (e.g., transferring a skill from practice to competition). What are some examples of when feedforward self-modeling may be useful for Kayla and Emma?

What Should Be in the Video/Demonstration? How Should It Be Presented?

The final two aspects of an observation-based intervention to address are, "What should I be watching … and how?"

Consider Kayla's goals of improving her race time and building confidence in her new technique. What demonstration content would be best suited to helping her reach each of those goals? To help you decide, consider the most important components of the task. For example, if you were teaching a young baseball player how to do an overarm throw, what would you want the key points to be? The wind-up? The preparatory step? Body rotation? The follow-through? The content of the demonstration should include the key elements for the task and the goals. In the case of Emma and her fear of the deep end, what would the key points of the demonstration be? As she is trying to overcome fear, consider the importance of psychological characteristics and how the model could demonstrate emotions and self-beliefs.

Now that you have chosen the content, select *how* you will present it. First, select the modality (i.e., a live model vs. video). Then, determine the best viewing angle, taking into consideration how Kayla would have the best view of the key points you want her to see. You may want to include more than one viewing angle. Next, identify the speed of the demonstration and the frequency with which you want Kayla to view it. Both of these factors may interact to determine the modality you will use. For example, if you want Kayla to view a video of her personal best race to date the night before a race, and again before competing, then a self-modeling video would be most appropriate.

From theories such as social learning theory (Bandura, 1986) and research on observational learning (see McCullagh, Law, & Ste-Marie, 2012 for a review), we know that modeling is often not used alone. Verbal or visual instructions, as well as verbal feedback, are instructional features frequently used to help draw the athlete's attention to the important parts of the demonstration, and to help them develop cue words or images that they can use as reminders when they are physically performing the task they observed. Imagine that you are Kayla's coach and are helping her with her technique. What instructions and feedback might you give her? How would you do this? Consider what aspects of the demonstration you would like her to focus on and how you will direct her attention to them.

Now, examine what you have filled into the diagram for Try It Out! Activity 1. Based on who you have selected as a model for Kayla, determine which modality is most feasible and appropriate for her situation. Traditionally, observational learning relied on live demonstrations; however, video-based demonstrations can now be easily created. Make sure you consider the practicality of when and where you would like Kayla to view the demonstration.

Uses of Modeling in Exercise and Rehabilitation

Now that you have explored how to design an observation intervention in a sport setting, let's think about how this technique could be applied to exercise and rehabilitation settings. There has been relatively little study of how viewing others or the self (i.e., in mirrors or on video) can be used to change our thoughts, feelings, and behaviour in these settings.

> ### Deep Thought
>
> Think of the last time you were exercising with other people around—maybe at the gym, in an exercise class, or running with friends. Did you watch anyone? If so, why? What were you paying attention to? With a partner, discuss how you use observation in an exercise setting.

Within Bandura's (1986, 1997) theories of social learning and self-efficacy, watching others is considered a powerful source of information and a basis for our self-beliefs, especially when we are faced with a new and challenging situation. Sustaining an injury and having to face physiotherapy could be one such situation. For people who are new to exercise or who are trying to get back into an active routine, watching others may help them to feel comfortable and build their exercise skills. We can approach these physical activity settings using the applied model for the use of observation in the same way that we used it to design observation experiences in sport.

Summary: Putting It All Together

Now that you have explored the factors that influence the effectiveness of observational learning in various physical activity settings, the last step is to apply that knowledge to the design of an intervention. Interventions can take many forms, but for modeling, video-based interventions are becoming more and more popular. Use your knowledge to design a video-based intervention to help an athlete, an exerciser, and an individual recovering from injury. Complete the Putting It All Together Activity on page 127 to test your knowledge.

Try It Out!

Activity 1: Planning a Modeling Intervention

Let's use Kayla's situation to help identify the key components of a modeling intervention tailored to her goals of improving her swim time and feeling more confident. Using the diagram below, fill in each of the blank boxes with the most important details. You may want to fill in the boxes separately for each of her desired outcomes. When you are done, you will see that you have created a guide you can follow when creating the actual live or video-based modeling experience for Kayla.

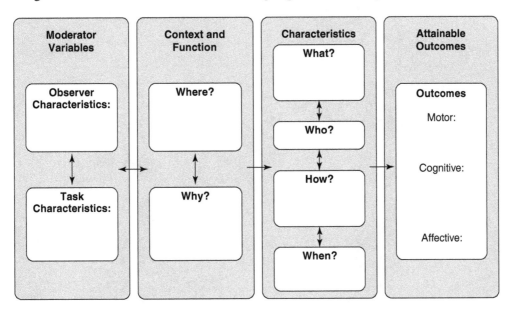

Name _____   Student No. _____

Activity 2: Identifying Key Model Characteristics

Based on Kayla's and Emma's scenarios, complete the following table. First, read over their scenarios and identify their key characteristics. Then, based on the athlete characteristics and desired outcomes, identify important model characteristics that will help them achieve their specific goals.

Athlete	Athlete Characteristics	Desired Outcome	Model Characteristics
Kayla (varsity swimmer)		Build confidence in technique	
Emma (young swimmer)		Reduce fear of deep end of the pool	

Putting It All Together Activity

In applied sport psychology, modeling interventions can take the form of a highlight video, created specifically for an athlete. Based on what you have learned about designing an observation-based intervention, use the same approach to plan a storyboard for how you would create a highlight video for each of the following scenarios. A storyboard is like a comic strip, showing frame by frame what the video will include visually, as well as any speech or music that will be included. Use the template on the following page to map out your video. You may want to make copies of the template to suit the length of your video or to complete the storyboard for a different scenario.

A. A team that wants to boost their confidence going into the playoffs.

B. An athlete who recently suffered a shoulder injury and has six months of physiotherapy to complete before he or she can return to sport.

C. A recreational athlete, who wants to boost his motivation to continue with his physically active lifestyle.

For your example, make sure to consider carefully *who* the best models should be, *what* you will show them saying and/or doing on the tape, *how* you will have them view the demonstration, the function (or *why*) the athlete is using the modeling video, and *when* and *where* the best opportunity is to show the video. If you think creating a series of videos is better than just one, map out those as well.

Scenario: _____

Scene #: _____

Script/Audio:

Scene #: _____

Script/Audio:

Scene #: _____

Script/Audio:

Scene #: _____

Script/Audio:

Scene #: _____

Script/Audio:

Scene #: _____

Script/Audio:

Suggested Readings and References

Bandura, A. (1986). *Social foundations of thought and action: A social cognitive theory.* Englewood Cliffs, NJ: Prentice-Hall.

Bandura, A. (1997). *Self-efficacy: The exercise of control.* New York: Freeman.

McCullagh, P., Law, B., & Ste-Marie, D. M. (in press). Chapter 13: The role of modeling on performance. In S. Murphy (Ed.), *The Oxford Handbook of Sport and Performance Psychology.* New York, NY: Oxford University Press.

Ste-Marie, D. M., Law, B., Rymal, A. M., O, J., Hall, C., & McCullagh, P. (2012). Observation interventions for motor skill learning and performance: An applied model for the use of observation. *International Review of Sport and Exercise Psychology.* DOI:10.1080/17509 84X.2012.665076

Chapter 9

United We Stand: Team Dynamics

Key Concepts and Theories

- Teams versus groups
- Group/team norms
- Roles
- Collective efficacy
- Team cohesion

Team Scenario

Laura is currently attending the first of several training camps with the National Wheelchair Basketball Team. The team is experiencing some growing pains as several veterans are no longer with the team, resulting in the addition of numerous rookies to the roster. Laura is a second-year player and is uncertain as to what her role is on the team. Several factors, such as the age gap between players (ages range from 20 to 50 years old), experience, personalities, skill level, and geographical location, have resulted in the development of cliques. Furthermore, in their first exhibition game, the team under-performed and players were clearly more concerned with their own individual statistics than the team's performance. The coach is seeking help to eliminate the "I" mindset and replace it with a more productive "WE" mentality.

Introduction

The case study nicely depicts the dynamic and complex nature of sport teams. The previous chapters have focused on individual concepts and have provided insightful applied techniques for the individual athlete. However, a large majority of sport is conducted within a team environment and requires an understanding of how groups function in order to help teams perform optimally. A team is a unique entity that is not simply the sum of its parts but rather a product of multiple variables and interactions. This chapter will explore various group constructs and provide practical solutions to common team problems.

© Lucian Coman, 2012. Used under license from Shutterstock, Inc.

What Is a Team?

As you have learned in your sport psychology class, a sport team is defined as "a collection of two or more individuals who possess a common identity, have common goals and objectives, share a common fate, exhibit structured patterns of interaction and modes of communication, hold common perceptions about the group structure, are personally and instrumentally interdependent, reciprocate interpersonal attraction, and consider themselves to be a group" (Carron, Hausenblas, & Eys, 2005, p. 13). These key components of a team are present regardless of sport, level, age, or gender. For example, members of a male youth recreational hockey team will have a common goal (e.g., to have fun) as will the national female basketball team (e.g., win the next Paralympics competition). The goals may differ, but the underlying concepts remain the same for every team.

As highlighted by the definition, teams are complex entities, and understanding what makes a team successful is no simple task. This is a fact realized by several professional teams who have allotted substantial resources to identifying and honing individual talent only to fail to win a championship. For instance, the 2011 Boston Red Sox spent millions of dollars around the concept of sabermetrics (i.e., statistics that measure individual player's in-game activity—a prime example is from the movie *MoneyBall*), yet the team suffered one of the most epic collapses in recent sport history. The general manger, Theo Epstein, did not blame the failure on statistics, but on the lack of team chemistry—a construct that has yet to be quantified by a mathematical formula. Consequently, it is necessary to conceptualize the key group constructs that influence team effectiveness in order to better help teams perform.

One of the most useful conceptual frameworks available to understand sport teams was developed by Carron and colleagues (2005). The framework consists of inputs, throughputs, and outputs. The inputs are composed of the attributes of the individual group members (e.g., age, skill level) and the nature of the team's environment (e.g., group size). The throughputs refer to the team's structure (e.g., norms, roles), processes (e.g., collective efficacy, goal setting), and cohesiveness. It is important to note that the throughputs—group structure, group processes, and group cohesion—have a reciprocal relationship. From the moment a group is formed the three constructs are at work influencing one another. Last, outputs are the consequences at both the individual (e.g., performance and adherence) and team (e.g., team outcome and group stability) level. The inputs influence the throughputs which ultimately influence the outputs. The remainder of this chapter will focus on the various *throughputs* (i.e., team structure, team processes, and team cohesiveness) as these are the variables that you can (directly or indirectly) influence, which will subsequently influence the team outputs of adherence and performance.

Team Structure

There are numerous constructs—group position, group status, group norms, and group role—that comprise a team's structure. A useful analogy is to think of the team structure as being similar to the foundation of a home—without a strong foundation a house would crumble. Similarly, without a strong foundation, a team will also crumble. Thus, it is crucial for coaches and athletes to develop a solid team structure to ensure consistent success and athlete satisfaction.

Deep Thought

Take a couple minutes to reflect on the structure of a team you to which you currently belong. What is your position? Are you a rookie or veteran? Are there specific behaviours expected of all team members (e.g., curfew, work ethic, game attire)? What is your role on the team? How do these variables influence your team's performance?

© Dmitriy Shironosov, 2012. Used under license from Shutterstock, Inc.

What Are Team Norms?

As you know, norms are the standards for behaviour that are expected of team members. In other words: team norms are the unwritten rules, implicit or explicit, that regulate an individual's behaviour within the team setting. There are two primary means by which team norms emerge—team interactions and reinforcement. We know that teams with higher levels of interpersonal interactions have a clearer understanding of the behaviours expected of its members, and thus, demonstrate higher levels of conformity (compared to teams with lower levels of interpersonal interactions). For instance, as a member of a basketball team Laura will have substantially more interpersonal interactions with her teammates and coaches than if she was a member of, say, a track and field team. Thus, simply because basketball teams have a greater degree of interaction compared to track and field teams, you can predict that, assuming all else is equal, a basketball team will demonstrate greater conformity than a track and field team. In addition to interactions, reinforcement is necessary for the emergence and effectiveness of norms. Behaviours that are deemed acceptable should be rewarded whereas unacceptable behaviours should be sanctioned.

Not surprisingly, team norms have been found to have a lasting effect on performance. Specifically, once norms have been established—positive or negative—they are transmitted to succeeding generations. For example, a team that has established several negative norms—being late for practice, showing poor work ethic on and off the court, being disrespectful to teammates and coaches—will endure the ramifications of these norms for several seasons to come, even when the initial members responsible for the emergence of the norms have been removed from the team. In fact, multiple sources have suggested that team norms have the potential lifespan of four to five seasons. As such, it is imperative that coaches and athletes take the steps necessary to establish positive norms to ensure a winning performance.

Complete Try It Out! Activity 1 on page 141 to identify and establish some team norms for your team. Notice that these Try It Out! activities in this chapter require the involvement of an entire team, and thus, may not be appropriate or feasible for some readers.

What Are Team Roles?

Roles are the pattern of behaviour expected of an individual in the team setting. An athlete's role on a team is formed by the combination of the individual's position, status, and/or assigned responsibilities (Carron et al., 2005). On any given team, athletes will have different roles that must be fulfilled in order for their team to be successful. For example, on an ice hockey team you will have a goal scorer, a play maker, and an enforcer, to name a few. All are essential to the team's success.

> ### Deep Thought
>
> Think of a team you belong to, what is your role? What are some other roles fulfilled by your teammates? What are some contributing factors to role emergence?

When discussing roles from an applied perspective, perhaps the most important issue to address is the need for congruency between an athlete and a coach's perspective of what the athlete's role is on the team. Role ambiguity is a common problem that can hinder performance. Beauchamp, Bray, Eys, and Carron (2002) developed a useful conceptual model of role ambiguity for interactive sport teams. The model proposes that athletes need to understand four aspects of their role in order to attain role clarity: scope of responsibilities, behaviours to fulfill responsibilities, evaluation of role performance, and consequences of not fulfilling responsibilities.

Let's examine how these components may result in role ambiguity with reference to our athlete Laura from the case study. In terms of scope of responsibilities, it is important for Laura to understand the general roles she is expected and required to perform. Perhaps she is required to be the backup point guard as well as the social leader off the court.

A second area requiring clarification is exactly how Laura is expected to carry out her defined responsibilities. Laura likely has a clear idea of what is required of her as a point guard but may be confused as to what behaviours are expected of her as a social leader. Laura may wonder, is a social leader basically the team clown? Is it someone who is vocal only in the locker room and silent on the court? This role is rather ambiguous in nature—especially for a younger player—causing potential problems if not clarified by the coaching staff.

A third possible source of role ambiguity involves understanding how role performance will be evaluated. In terms of Laura's task role (point guard), will she be evaluated on her stats or her effort? As a backup point guard she likely will not see many minutes. In order to maintain her confidence it is crucial that she understand how playing minutes are determined. Likewise, how will the coaches assess her social role? Will her ability to lead off court translate to playing time?

Last, Laura may endure some role ambiguity if she is uncertain as to what the consequences are for not successfully fulfilling her roles. Will she be benched if she makes a bad pass? If she fails to increase social cohesion among her teammates will she be reprimanded? Laura's situation depicts how a coach's failure to clarify these four components of an athlete's role could result in role ambiguity, which may lead to a decrease in motivation and confidence, and ultimately a decrease in performance. Considering the multitude of factors that must be considered with regard to role clarity it is of value to review two interventions that may help reduce role ambiguity.

Complete Try It Out! Activity 2 on page 143 with your team to help increase role clarity among your team members.

Group Processes

Group processes consist of constructs such as attributions, interaction and communications, group goal setting, and collective efficacy. Not surprisingly, research has found a link between group processes and performance.

Perhaps one of the most essential group processes in terms of team success is collective efficacy. *Collective efficacy* is defined as a team's belief in its ability to successfully execute various tasks related to performance. Unfortunately, a team's efficacy sometimes waivers and performance suffers until the team regains belief in its ability. Several strategies have been covered through lectures or in your textbook, which are known to increase collective efficacy. These may include reflection on positive past performances, use of vicarious experiences (i.e., observing a subjectively similar team achieve success), use of verbal persuasion, effective group leadership, manipulation of group size, and increase of group cohesion.

One additional way to increase collective efficacy, team interactions, and team communication is team goal setting. In Chapter 2 we explained in detail the key components of individual goal setting as well as the process of performance profiling. This intervention can easily be adapted to the team level and will have favourable results on a team's motivation, focus, team efficacy, and cohesiveness. The following is a simple method to conduct a team goal-setting session:

Step 1: Educate the athletes on the importance of setting team goals and the SMART principles.
Step 2: Divide the team into smaller groups (either by position, mixed status, or randomly). Each subgroup will have 10 to 15 minutes to discuss and complete a team performance profile handout.
Step 3: Each subgroup will verbalize to their teammates the five key attributes they believe a championship team must possess. The subgroup will also note which of the attributes they identified as needing the most work with regard to their team.

Step 4: After hearing from each subgroup, the team as a whole will decide on the top three attributes that need immediate attention and are crucial to their team's success.

Step 5: These three attributes will become the focus of the team's short-term goals. The team will use the SMART goal-setting principles to establish three team goals based on the results of the performance profiling.

Step 6: The goals will be written down and posted in the locker room.

Step 7: Team goals will be evaluated constantly from game to game and practice to practice.

Step 8: Team goals will be adjusted when necessary.

Team Cohesion

> *"In the past players asked 'Where do I fit in? How can I help this team win?' Now they ask: 'How do I get what I want?' Given this selfish mindset, it is remarkable actually that teams play with any cohesiveness ... Good teams become great ones when the members trust each other enough to surrender the 'me' for the 'we.' Individuals are required to surrender their self-interest for the greater good so that the whole adds up to more than the sums of the part."*
>
> –(Jackson, 2004, p. 25).

Team cohesion is probably one of the most cited topics with regard to group dynamics. As noted above, the great NBA coach Phil Jackson articulated both the importance of cohesion and also the difficulty in cultivating cohesion in today's ego-centric environment. You can likely think of many sport failures that have been attributed to a lack of team chemistry and several championships won by teams with less individual talent but more team chemistry. In fact, researchers have been able to provide empirical support for the old adage that championships are won by teams not by individuals.

Thus, cohesion is undeniably an important construct for any sport team to foster. As a player, coach, or sport psychology consultant it is important to understand what cohesion is and what variables are correlated with the construct. Cohesion is defined as "a dynamic process which is reflected in the tendency for a group to stick together and remain united in the pursuit of its instrumental objectives and/or for the satisfaction of member affective needs" (Carron, Brawley, & Widmeyer, 1998, p. 123). Two key aspects to keep in mind are that cohesion is dynamic and multidimensional. The dynamic nature of cohesion refers to the fact that cohesion changes over time. A team's cohesiveness generally changes from the beginning of the season to playoff time. The multidimensional nature of cohesion refers to the two different types of cohesion: task and social. With regard to Laura's team, an example of task cohesion would be the team being united in achieving their goal of qualifying for the next Paralympics. In contrast, the presence of cliques on Laura's team and the lack of friendships and social interactions off the court reflect low social cohesion. Both have been found to be important for team success (Carron et al., 2002).

Several factors have been found to influence a team's task and social cohesion. Specifically, the variables fall within four categories: environmental (e.g., proximity, group size), leadership (e.g., decision-making style, social support behaviour), personal (e.g., attributions, state anxiety, adherence behaviour), and team factors (e.g., role involvement, team norms, collective efficacy). It is important to note that the relationship between these numerous factors and cohesion is reciprocal in nature. For additional information on the research concerning the relationship between cohesion and the above mentioned factors, refer to Carron et al.'s (2005) book entitled *Group Dynamics in Sport*.

Evidently, developing team cohesion is pivotal to a team's success. Unfortunately, there is no foolproof recipe that ensures team chemistry. However, there are several team-building activities/interventions that can facilitate the development of team cohesiveness. One useful resource to use when creating team-building interventions is Carron and Spink's (1993) conceptual model of the factors that influence a team's cohesiveness. The model is linear in nature and proposes that both the team structure (e.g., role clarity, team norms) and team environment (e.g., proximity) will influence team processes (e.g., team goals, collective efficacy). In turn, team processes will influence the cohesiveness of the team. For example, with regard to Laura's team, having a centralized training camp and establishing role clarity would likely result in a greater commitment and achievement of the team's goals resulting in higher collective efficacy and ultimately an increase in team unity. The key is identifying what factors require immediate attention and developing an effective game plan. Similar to when working with individual athletes, it is crucial to individualize team-building interventions to the team's needs. Remember: regardless of whether the intervention is at the individual or team level, there is no-one-size-fits-all when it comes to the development and application of any sport psychology intervention.

Below are just a few strategies that have been found to increase task and social cohesion amongst sport teams:

- **Team Goal Setting**. Helps increase focus, motivation, and team unity. Refer to section on group processes.
- **Establish Team Norms**. Refer to Try It Out! Activity 1.
- **Role Clarity**. Refer to roles section and the "Hot Seat" (Try it Out! Activity 2).
- **Create a Team Identity**. Enhance the team's distinctiveness by having them wear the same tracksuit to events. Some teams will create a slogan for their team and have it printed on T-shirts that they wear during warm-up.
- **Team Dinners/Social Events**. An excellent way for athletes to spend time together off the court and develop social cohesion.
- **Workout Buddy System**. You can pair a rookie with a veteran player to reduce the existence of cliques. The pair is responsible for each other's off-court training and will increase player accountability.
- **Centralized Training Camps**. When creating a national program it is crucial that athletes attend several centralized training camps to allow them an opportunity to bond with fellow teammates on and off the court. Perhaps the best evidence validating this philosophy can be seen from the success of the Women's Team Canada Ice Hockey Team. The team had several training camps throughout the year leading up to the 2010 Winter Olympics where athletes were required to live in a remote area together and endure intensive on- and off-ice training to increase both task and social cohesion. The team was successful in achieving their outcome goal of winning the Olympic gold medal.
- **Ropes Activity**. There is likely a ropes course in your community that tailors to team building activities for teams. This activity forces athletes to work together as a unit and develop trust in

their teammates. Most teams who do a ropes course will do it at the beginning of the season to help athletes bond.

- **Most Valuable Player of the Game Award**. Several teams have adopted a unique way to reward a teammate who played a significant role in their team's winning performance. The premise is simple: following every win the previous MVP awards the player who most contributed to the team's win with a trophy to hold onto until the next win. The award is not designed to recognize individual accomplishments but rather to identify a teammate who performs with the team's interests in mind (i.e., sacrificing "I" for "We"). For example, the Washington Capitals would award their MVP with a hard hat. The Capitals emphasized that the hard hat was given to a player who made a difference at the team level, not necessarily the player with the most points. A defense with four blocks that influenced the outcome would be just as viable a candidate as the center who scored a hat trick. Players are asked to give speeches and they have their name put on the hat, thus increasing team bonding. Several other professional and university teams have adopted a similar activity with a different reward (e.g., Boston Bruins—old sport coat bought on eBay; Wilfrid Laurier University Men's Hockey—24-karat golden hammer made by the players).

Summary: Putting It All Together

Teams are composed of individuals; because of this there are many group and personal variables that influence the effectiveness of the group. Constructs such as group structure, norms, and roles, among others, contribute to the development of the group and ultimately of the group's success in sport. Think of how you could facilitate group development by completing the Putting It All Together Activity 1 on page 145.

We have just discussed several ways to develop cohesion in sport teams. Some cohesion will develop naturally, because team members have regular contact with each other and are interested in playing their sport. There are times, of course, when it is helpful to boost task or social cohesion through team-building activities. Complete Putting It All Together Activity 2 on page 147 to test your understanding of how teams form.

Try It Out!

Activity 1: Team Norms Intervention

An effective intervention regarding team norms involves having athletes create a code of conduct or a team covenant that will outline the expected group behaviours for the members. This intervention can be done either directly (with a sport psychology consultant) or indirectly (the consultant will educate the coaching staff on the steps for the intervention). In order for the code of conduct to be effective it is essential that the athletes are active participants in the process. That is, a coach cannot simply create a list of rules and expect athletes to accept and adhere to them. If the team as a whole has ownership over the norms there will be a higher likelihood of conformity.

Creating a team code of conduct requires a team meeting with all the players and coaches present. The first step is to divide the team into subgroups. It is beneficial to have a mix of veterans and rookies within these subgroups to eliminate the possibility of cliques and to ensure different points of views are discussed. A by-product of this activity is an assist to promoting interactions between all team members and enhancing team unity. The subgroups will create a list of key team behaviours that are necessary for the team to be successful. For example, teams may list the following as required behaviours: good work ethic, respect for teammates and coaches, punctuality, commitment to off-court training, and other behaviours. Teams can list behaviours expected from athletes as well as from the coaching staff.

The second step involves the team reconvening as a whole with each subgroup writing its top five required team behaviours on a whiteboard. As a team, the athletes and coaches will narrow down the list to the top 10 norms or behaviours (or less—it is up to the team's discretion) that are imperative to the team's performance. In addition it is important for the team to discuss the ramifications for not adhering to the agreed-upon code of conduct. As noted earlier, norms are effective when the appropriate behaviours are reinforced and undesired behaviours are sanctioned; thus, the athletes and coaching staff must make a conscious effort to enforce the norms at all times in order for them to have a positive influence on performance.

The final step is to create a document listing the final team-generated norms or behaviours. Each team member and coach is required to sign the team code of conduct indicating a commitment to conform to the outlined norms. Some teams find it helpful to have one master copy of the code of conduct—signed by all the players and coaches— posted in the team locker room as a reminder and source of motivation. By signing the code of conduct team members are not only indicating they understand the team norms but also that they are committed fully to the team. Perhaps more importantly, the code of conduct increases accountability among the athletes and coaches. For example, if fitness training is on the code of conduct and Laura fails to complete her off-court training her teammates have the right to respectfully discuss her violation of one of the agreed-upon team norms. When executed properly, a code of conduct can help create and maintain positive team norms that help generate a solid team structure that will ultimately result in successful performance.

Try It Out!

Activity 2: Roles Intervention

An intervention that aids athletes' understanding of their role is referred to as the "Hot Seat." The Hot Seat has been found to increase role clarity, team and self-efficacy, and team cohesion. This intervention can be executed either by the coaching staff or a sport psychology consultant. In order for the Hot Seat to be effective it is important that team members are mature, respectful, and capable of receiving and giving constructive criticism.

The team sits in a circle and there is one seat, the Hot Seat, placed in the middle of the circle. Each athlete has the opportunity to sit in the Hot Seat where he or she is required to explain to the team his or her role and to list three positive skills or qualities they bring to the team and one area he or she needs to work on in order to help the team's performance. Once the athlete has listed his or her qualities, each teammate will be asked to provide a couple of positive skills the athlete brings to the team and one area the athlete could work on. All the athletes and coaches are required to contribute during this activity.

It is beneficial for the sport psychology consultant to record each player's comments and create a summary sheet with the athlete's top three qualities and one area of improvement that is positively worded. Some athletes find it useful to have their individual summary sheet in their locker stall to refer to prior to games. An alternate version of the Hot Seat—if time is limited or athletes are young or sensitive—is to have teammates anonymously write down their thoughts regarding their fellow team member's role and skill set. Both versions of this intervention have been shown to be very effective in clarifying team roles, increasing self and team confidence, and team unity.

Putting It All Together

Activity 1: Group Development

It is thought that group development occurs in sequential stages. Specifically, Tuckman (1965) proposed that all groups go through four key phases of development: *forming*, *storming*, *norming*, and *performing*. The first phase involves becoming familiar with teammates and determining the group's task and how to achieve it. The second phase is characterized by tension and conflict between team members revolving around how to carry out team tasks. The third stage is where cohesiveness begins to develop and team members start to adopt a "WE" mentality. Finally, the fourth phase focuses on group productivity and performance.

Laura's team is clearly still in the forming stage. What would be some ways to help her team move through each stage and ultimately get to the performing stage? Think of key things the coach and players can do to move from one stage to the next. Specifically, how would you get the team to move from the storming stage to the norming and ultimately the performing stage?

Putting It All Together

Activity 2: Team Building

This chapter focused on how to increase team and individual performance by the implementation of several different interventions for various group constructs. Now it is your turn to put on your sport psychology consultant hat and develop a team-building exercise for Laura's team. Make sure to identify what group construct(s) your intervention will address and clearly outline step by step how to carry out your team-building exercise.

Suggested Readings and References

Beauchamp, M. R., Bray, S. R., Eys, M. A., and Carron, A.V. (2002). Role ambiguity, role efficacy, and role performance: Multidimensional and mediational relationships within interdependent sport teams. *Group dynamics: Theory, research, and practice, 6,* 229–242.

Carron, A. V., Brawley, L. R., & Widmeyer, W. N. (1998). The measurement of cohesiveness in sport groups. In J. L. Duda (Ed.), *Advances in sport and exercise psychology measurement* (pp. 213–226). Morgantown, WV: Fitness Information Technology.

Carron, A. V., Colman, M. M., Wheeler, J., & Stevens, D. (2002). Cohesion and performance in sport: A meta-analysis. *Journal of Sport & Exercise Psychology, 24,* 168–188.

Carron, A. V., Hausenblas, H. A., & Eys, M. A. (2005). *Group dynamics in sport* (3rd ed.). Morgantown, WV: Fitness Information Technology.

Carron, A. V., & Spink, K. S. (1993). Team building in an exercise setting. *The Sport Psychologist, 7,* 8–18.

Colman, M. M. & Carron, A. V. (2001). The nature of norms in individual sport teams. *Small Group Research, 32,* 206–222.

Jackson, P. (2004). *The last season: A team in search of its soul.* New York: Hyperion.

Tuckman, B. W. (1965). Developmental sequences in small groups. *Psychological Bulletin, 63,* 384–399.

Zaccaro, S. J., Blair, V., Peterson, C., & Zazanis, M. (1995). Collective efficacy. In J. E. Maddux (Ed.), *Self-efficacy, adaptation, and adjustment: Theory, research, and application* (pp. 305–328). New York: Plenum Press.

Chapter 10

Communication

Key Concepts and Theories

- Message sending: verbal and nonverbal messages
- Message reception: listening styles (arrogant, superficial, active)
- Message interpretation: personal and contextual factors influencing message interpretation

Ashley is in a meeting with Coach Wilson, her high school volleyball coach. During the last few weeks Ashley has been putting out even more effort than usual on the court, trying to be a bigger contributor to the team in an attempt to "soften up" Coach for some news she is about to share: Ashley plans to tell Coach that she does not plan to return to the team next season due to her decision to specialize in curling in preparation for the Canada Games.

Ashley: *Hi Coach, thanks for meeting with me. There's something I wanted to talk to you about.*
Coach: *No worries. I think I know what it is. We should talk about it.*
Ashley: *Oh—really?*
Coach: *Yah, I've noticed you've really been busting your hump lately in practices. I think I know what's up.*
Ashley: *Well, I have been working harder, but—*
Coach: *[interrupting Ashley] I know, and you've proved your point. I'd like to make you an assistant captain for next year's squad. You really impressed me these last few weeks, I think you'll be a great leader. Congratulations.*
Ashley: *Oh. . . .um. . .thanks.*

The meeting ends without Ashley communicating to her coach that she does not plan to return next season. This vignette depicts a situation that is, perhaps, all too common in sport: poor communication. Ashley was not able to communicate her intended message to her coach, for a variety of reasons, which will be discussed later on.

Deep Thought

Chat with a few of your classmates and come up with a definition of *communication*. What does communication actually mean? How does one distinguish effective, from ineffective, communication?

Communication

As you have learned in class and from your course textbook, communication is not just talking. Similarly, effective communication is not just speaking clearly and directly. Certainly, this is *one part* of effective communication, but being an effective speaker alone, does not equate to being an effective communicator. Communication comprises three phases: (1) sending a message, (2) receiving a message, and (3) interpreting a message. Errors in communication can occur at any one, or in any combination, of these levels.

In the opening vignette, several communication errors are evident. First, Ashley made an error in *sending* her message as she did not actually state the message she wanted her coach to receive (that she would not be returning to the team). Second, Ashley's coach made an error in *receiving* the message, in that she used arrogant listening (i.e., the coach was more interested in getting her own message across, rather than taking the time to actually receive Ashley's message). Last, there was an error in *interpreting* Ashley's message. In this specific situation, the error in interpretation was actually due to Ashley's failure to *send* her intended message effectively; however, note that this is not always the case—errors in interpretation can be driven by errors on the part of the message sender *or* the message receiver.

Sending Effective Messages

You have learned some characteristics of effective and ineffective message sending from your course textbook and lectures. It is important to remember that a sent message is made up of both verbal and nonverbal messages. Message-sending problems can arise due to a variety of errors, and sometimes can be due to something as simple as content omission. Consider our vignette above: Ashley made an error in *sending* her message as she did not actually state the message she wanted her coach to receive (that she would not be returning to the team). More often than not, however, errors in communication are not so simple and unidimensional.

For example, a coach watches his athlete miss a game-winning free throw. During the break before overtime, the coach decides to talk to the athlete to keep the athlete calm, focused, and motivated to continue play. The coach walks over to the athlete, who, understandably, is hanging his head and staring at the ground. The coach begins by saying with an exasperated sigh: "It's ok, Pete—", and then adds in a empathetic tone: "You took your time on the shot, and lined it up well—sometimes you just don't get the lucky bounce". This is one example of an ineffectively sent message.

Although the coach's intentions were good, his message sending behaviours were bad (i.e., ineffective) because his choices of verbal and nonverbal messages did not accurately reflect his intentions. Using the words "It's ok" in a situation where an athlete has interpreted that he has just failed implies (or, in this case, *confirms*) that the athlete has failed. Though this may be true in an objective sense, sending this information to the athlete at this time does nothing to convey the *intended* message from the coach. In addition, the nonverbal message sent via the exasperated sigh might be interpreted by the athlete as meaning that the coach is disappointed or even angry with him. Last, in saying "sometimes you just don't get the lucky bounce" sends the message that free throws are, at least sometimes, out of the control of the athlete. This is an inaccurate statement; in basketball, the athlete *can* typically control all aspects of the free throw. This implied suggestion—that some free throws are out of one's control—may reduce an athlete's motivation toward free throw shooting (i.e., it may elicit a "why bother?" attitude), or may increase an athlete's anxiety by increasing his or her perceptions of uncontrollability over the situation (i.e., "I can do everything right and the free throw *still* might not go in"). Decreasing motivation and increasing anxiety were not the intentions of the coach in sending his message to his athlete, yet, due to ineffective message sending, these may be the outcomes of the message that was received and interpreted.

Deep Thought

Watch 20 to 30 minutes of your favorite sport film. In particular, pay attention to meaningful verbal exchanges between the various main characters in the film. Think about what you have learned about effective and ineffective message-sending behaviours and attempt to evaluate how effectively the actors and actresses are sending their messages. Note specific message-sending behaviours that you think are effective, as well as ones that you think are ineffective. In addition, explain why you think each behaviour is effective or ineffective with respect to sending the intended message.

In the free throw example above, it is clear that sending effective messages is not just about choosing your words effectively. When you send a message, you send information related to content, to your perceptions of the situation at hand, and to your emotions. It is important to first consider the exact message you want to send, and then, carefully choose not only your words, but also your nonverbal behaviours you will display when delivering that message. To optimize the effectiveness of your message, all three of these aspects of message sending must accurately represent your intended message!

Complete Try It Out! Activity 1 on page 159 to see how well you understand and can identify effective versus ineffective message-sending behaviours.

Receiving Messages Effectively

As already noted, effective communication is not only about being able to send effective messages. A second component of being an effective communicator involves being able to effectively *receive* messages. Consider Ashley's coach in the opening vignette. The coach is demonstrating poor message reception skills. The coach is not actually listening to Ashley: she cuts Ashley off in the middle of her message transmission (i.e., she does not let her finish her sentences). This can be a common message reception error for people who employ the least-effective type of listening, *arrogant listening*. As you have likely learned in lecture or in reading your course textbook, when people employ arrogant listening, they do not actually have an interest in hearing what the other person has to say, rather, they want to push their own agenda and operate under their a priori assumptions regarding the message that the message sender is trying to transmit (e.g., the coach says to Ashley: "I think I know what it is," in reference to the message Ashley is trying to communicate to her coach). In these situations—where the message receiver assumes she or her already knows what the message sender is going to say—the receiver does not attend to the actual message being sent, she or he is merely looking for an opportunity to start speaking. Unfortunately this can lead to misinterpretation and miscommunication, as well as frustration and perhaps even resentment on the part of the message sender. When arrogant listening prevails, effective communication cannot exist.

The other types of listening that you have probably learned about are superficial listening and active listening. During *superficial listening* (or point-form listening), message receivers only attend to keywords or phrases that allow them to come up with what they *think* is the meaning of the message being sent. In attending to only certain words or phrases and "tuning out" others, the message receiver increases his or her sense of certainty of their *assumed* meaning of the message, without actually listening to the *entire* message. This means that although the basic meaning of the message may be understood, underlying factors or emotions may not be accurately received or interpreted by the message receiver. For example, in the opening vignette, the coach commends Ashley on her recent increase in her effort during volleyball practice and competition. In response to the coach's compliment, Ashley confirms that she has been putting out more effort. However, rather than listening to Ashley's *entire* message, the coach takes Ashley's confirmation of her increased effort on the court as confirmation of an a priori assumption: "Ashley is working hard because she wants to be a leader on this team." The coach doesn't consider that there may be other factors driving her increased effort.

Even if one's assumptions are correct, superficial listening is still not an optimal listening style as the message receiver is not allowing the message sender a chance to accurately evaluate the effectiveness of his or her sent message. This can lead to communication issues in the future, as the message sender will not know whether he or she effectively communicated the intended message (and thus, cannot make changes to improve his or her message-sending behaviours). In addition, superficial listening, similar to arrogant listening, may lead message senders to become frustrated or resentful of the message receiver, to the point where he or she chooses to completely disengage during further communications (e.g., "Why bother; he is not listening to me, anyway").

The most effective listening style is *active listening*. When people are actively listening, they are truly engaged in message reception: they allow the message sender time to deliver the entire message *without interruption*, they consider the message sender's emotions and nonverbal behaviours when interpreting the sent message, and they confirm with the message sender that their understanding of the sent message is accurate *before* responding to the message (refer to your course textbook for specific examples of effective message reception behaviours). In short, active listening involves demonstrating to the message sender that you are interested in, and care about, achieving an accurate understanding of the message that the sender is trying to transmit to you. Although active listening sounds easy in theory, it can be an onerous task for some. Just think of how many conversations you have been in where interruptions to the message sender abound. At its worst, this can lead to a back-and-forth pattern of broken sentences, as if each participant is trying to "one up" the other by demonstrating superior knowledge or understanding of a topic or situation.

Deep Thought

Think of a time where you were having a conversation with someone, and got the very distinct feeling that that person was not listening to you. Now that you have learned that there are, in fact, several listening styles, it is possible that the person was listening to you but was not using the most effective listening style. Reflect on this conversation you have recalled, and try to determine what style of listening that person was using by analyzing his or her message reception behaviours during your conversation.

Complete Try It Out! Activity 2 on page 161 to practice the skill of identifying errors in communication related to message reception.

Interpreting Messages Effectively

Many times, personal biases or beliefs regarding a situation or a general topic may lead us to create a priori assumptions or premature conclusions regarding the message being sent. Sometimes, these assumptions or premature conclusions can even lead to our interruption of the message sender during the transmission of his or her message. For example, in the opening vignette, Ashley's coach had an a priori assumption (i.e., personal belief) that, if a volleyball player puts forth increased effort, this automatically means that she is highly motivated to play the sport. Although this may often be the case, it was not the case in Ashley's situation. Because the coach did not employ active listening skills, her personal belief (paired with Ashley's ineffective message transmission) lead to an inaccurate *interpretation* of the sent message.

It is best to leave most personal biases and beliefs out of any communication. This is because personal biases and beliefs will influence how one interprets their own world; however, when you are trying to understand a message being sent to you by *other people*, you need to understand *their world*, not yours!

Unless the other person's biases and beliefs are *exactly identical* to your own, imposing your biases and beliefs on the message sender's message may not only be inappropriate, but may also lead to misinterpretation of the sent message.

Deep Thought

Discuss with a classmate, teammate, or friend whether you believe that certain personal biases are more difficult to leave out of message reception and interpretation than others. If yes, what are some examples of these more robust personal biases, and *why* do you think they are so difficult to leave out of communication? Last, discuss whether you think these personal biases should be left out of communications in the first place, and if so, how one might try to increase his or her success in doing so.

So what, how does/will one know if a personal bias or belief will have an influence on communication behaviours? This question, like many questions surrounding the psychology of human behaviour and cognition, does not have a simple answer. The answer is dependent on a variety of personal and contextual factors. The interplay of these factors with the message sender, message receiver, and even with each other (i.e., interactions between factors) can influence how a message is sent, received, and ultimately, interpreted by the message receiver.

For example, an athlete with low sport-confidence (a personal factor) may hold a strong *personal belief* that they are not physically skilled at their sport. If the athlete *chooses* to allow this personal belief (i.e., "I am *not* skilled") to influence their message reception and/or interpretation skills, he or she will likely be inaccurate in interpreting any message that is intended to mean: "You *are* physically skilled." Interestingly, this misinterpretation would likely occur regardless of the degree of effectiveness of the message transmission behaviours! This is because the athlete has *allowed* his or her personal belief (i.e., "I am not skilled") to influence his or her message reception skills, and thus, the athlete will either employ arrogant or superficial listening (rather than active listening). This, in turn, causes the athlete to disregard the sent message altogether (arrogant listening), or, to interpret the message to mean something else, such as: "you are good at 'this' part of the skill, but *bad* at all of the other parts of the skill that I haven't mentioned" (superficial listening). From this example, you have probably realized that ineffective communication happens more often than we may think.

It is important to understand that the influence of personal factors (e.g., personality traits, previous experiences, upbringing, religion, values, etc.) on one's message sending, receiving, and/or interpretation skills can actually be controlled by the person in which the personal factor resides. These factors do not "have to" come into play during communication; their influence is *not* inevitable. The individual can consciously *choose* to regulate the influence of personal factors during communications, although typically, many of us do not think to do this during normal, day-to-day interactions with others. If one does not consciously choose to regulate the influence of certain personal factors (or, consciously chooses to allow influence of certain personal factors) then one should expect that their personal beliefs and biases will exert at least some influence on their communication with others. This is not to say that allowing personal factors to exist unregulated is inherently bad, we are merely suggesting that, in some situations, regulation of certain personal factors may be beneficial in increasing the effectiveness of your interpersonal communications.

For example, a middle school volleyball coach who holds extremely high expectations of herself regarding physical fitness may consciously choose to regulate these personal beliefs (i.e., "to me, being fit means . . .") such that they are not influencing her message transmissions regarding physical fitness to her young athletes. Imposing her personal biases regarding the definition of physical fitness may be inappropriate for this specific population as her biases are based on her own personal experiences with, and level of, physical fitness. In this situation, it would probably be more appropriate for the coach to gain an accurate understanding of what the definition of physical fitness is for a middle-school athlete or even for a middle-school child in general, and use that information to inform her choices of what messages to send regarding physical fitness.

It is not just personal factors that can influence interpersonal communication. Many contextual factors can also play a role in how one may send, receive, or interpret a message. Contextual factors are essentially any factor that exists during a specific interpersonal communication. These types of factors differ from personal factors in that personal factors are not situation-specific; personal factors will always be present in any given interpersonal communication (e.g., values, religion, personality traits, etc.; one can choose whether to regulate relevant personal factors). Contextual factors, on the other hand, will vary depending on the various things making up the specific situation one finds him- or herself in.

For example, a high school sprinter may find himself feeling extremely anxious when speaking to a potential college coach in the coach's office about his sprinting, but perfectly calm when speaking to his high school coach in his home locker room about the same topic. Here, the obvious contextual factors are feelings of anxiety, the environment (unfamiliar vs. familiar), and the sprinter's relationship with the other person (potential college coach vs. current high school coach); however, there may be other contextual factors that would only be identifiable if more information were provided (e.g., trust, power, or control issues, self-efficacy issues, feelings of intimidation, etc.).

Generally speaking, contextual factors can be related to one's: perceptions regarding the specific situation they are in, current mental state, current environment, relationships with others, and, current social milieu (e.g., certain cultural norms and/or rules). Just like personal factors, contextual factors can influence how we send, receive, or interpret messages. In the preceding example with the sprinter speaking to the potential college coach, the anxiety the sprinter is feeling may have a negative influence on his ability to accurately send nonverbal aspects of certain messages (e.g., "I am a confident athlete"; "I belong here"; etc.). Additionally, the anxiety may lead to less effective listening and/or message interpretation skills. It is also possible that the sprinter's relationship with the potential coach may influence various aspects of communication. If one is less comfortable with another person or if there is an element of distrust (or at least uncertainty), sent messages may be more factual (than personal), and message reception and interpretation may be more easily influenced by personal factors. Last, the sprinter's choice of what (and what *not*) to communicate to the coach may be influenced by the sprinter's perceptions of the cultural norms for college-level sprinters. For example, the sprinter may assume that one norm is that college sprinters must demonstrate detailed knowledge of the skill and of training methods; thus, the athlete may choose to use a great deal of jargon and reference to various training methods in an attempt to demonstrate that they can meet this cultural norm.

Another possibility to consider is that various factors may interact with each other, and this interaction may then influence communication in some way. For example, a skilled golfer who has a dispositional tendency to become highly anxious in unfamiliar situations (a personal factor related to personality) may have great difficulty speaking to his teammates during a charity event, if placed on a team of individuals with whom the golfer is unfamiliar (a contextual factor). In this example, the combination of the golfer's personality and the specific situation he is in works together to negatively influence communication (poor message sending). As you can see, sometimes, the causes of communication errors can be quite complex. However, in gaining a clearer understanding of the possible causes of communication errors (as well as how to communicate effectively) you can begin to increase the effectiveness of your interpersonal communication skills.

Complete Try It Out! Activity 3 on page 163 to evaluate personal and contextual factors that may influence how you might interpret messages sent to you by others in your sport.

Summary: Putting It All Together

As we have discussed and have encouraged you to think about in this chapter, communication is not as simple as speaking clearly and honestly. Since there are at least two individuals involved in any interpersonal communication, you must consider the various roles involved in any conversation between two people: message sending, message receiving, and message interpretation. If you are looking to improve your communication skills it is a good idea to begin by reflecting on your own communication skills to identify any areas that may need improvement or modification. However, always remember that human interaction involves more than just one person, and thus, it may also be beneficial to reflect on the communication strengths and weaknesses of those with whom you regularly interact! Identifying communication strengths and weaknesses in others may allow you to help those individuals improve upon their communication skills, and it will also allow you to gain a better understanding of the possible causes of communication breakdowns you experience with those individuals. Improve your own communication skills by completing the Putting It All Together activity in this chapter.

Try It Out!

Activity 1: Do "this," not "that": Identifying effective and ineffective message sending behaviours

Observe one of your coaches as he or she gives feedback to other athletes during practice. Try to identify effective and ineffective message-sending behaviours on the part of your coach. Later, after practice, write down the message-sending behaviours you observed of your coach in two columns, labeling one column as "effective" and the other as "ineffective" message-sending behaviours.

Next, reflect on your own message-sending behaviours when communicating with that same coach. Perform the same task, identifying both "effective" and "ineffective" message-sending behaviours that you perform when communicating with your coach. If you find any message-sending behaviour that you (or your coach) performs consistently, you may choose to address this behaviour in order to improve your message-sending skills. You can also do the same exercise with your teammates, evaluating how effectively you send messages to each other.

Try It Out!

Activity 2: There's an 'I' in 'I'm Not Listening': Ineffective versus Effective Message Reception Behaviours

You will need a partner for this three-part activity. For the first part, choose one person to be the message sender and the other to be the message receiver. The message receiver should give the message sender a few minutes to write out a very brief three-paragraph "story" about him- or herself, one that he or she knows you are not already familiar with (don't spend too much time, here—five minutes, tops). The story will be about a goal he or she has recently pursued, sport-related or not (e.g., adding lean mass, buying a new outfit, earning a starting position, impressing others at a job interview, etc.).

Here is some information to help structure the story:

- First paragraph: Introduce all characters in the story and the goal your partner was trying to accomplish.
- Second paragraph: Describe the action in the story. The 'action' will be the description of the things done to pursue that goal (e.g., reducing Calorie intake, going to the mall, increasing batting cage swings, etc.).
- Third paragraph: The conclusion of the story. This should be a description of the outcome of the 'action'.

Once the story is ready, instruct your partner to begin telling you the story. As he or she is sending his or her message (i.e., telling you his or her "story"), perform message reception skills that you know to be associated with the *arrogant listening style*. You may find it helpful to review your lecture or textbook notes before starting if you can't quite remember the types of behaviours associated with the arrogant listening style.

Once your partner is finished sending his or her message, take a *maximum of one minute* to create a bullet-point summary of the major points from your partner's story. You should have bullet points for each paragraph of the story. While you are doing this, your partner should take this time to record a few of the behaviours that you performed that he or she found made telling you the story difficult, frustrating, and/or unenjoyable. Set these notes aside, and do not share them with each other.

Now, switch roles. You become the message sender, and your partner, the message receiver. Since there are three parts to this activity, you and your partner can both take up to five minutes to write a story about a goal each of you have pursued recently. Follow the same guidelines your partner used above to write these stories.

Once the two stories are complete, have your partner (who is now the message receiver) set his or her story aside for the time being. Instruct your partner to adopt behaviours known to be associated with the *superficial listening style*. Begin telling your partner your story. Once you have gotten through your story, have your partner spend a *maximum of one minute* creating a bullet-point summary of the major points of your story (with bullet points for each paragraph), as you take down some notes regarding behaviours that made it challenging, difficult, or unenjoyable to tell your story.

Now switch roles one more time (you become the message receiver, again) and have your partner read his or her next story to you, however, this time perform behaviours associated with the *active listening style*. Perform the same summary task.

Now that you have experimented with all three listening styles, work with your partner and review your notes for each listening style. In particular, (1) compare the accuracy and comprehensiveness of the summary of the major points for each story (compare to the actual story that was written out); and (2) create a summary list of the behaviours you found to hinder communication, in general (i.e., you do not need to separate this list by listening styles). Once this is completed, write a brief summary of what you have learned from this activity regarding effective and ineffective listening styles.

Try It Out!

Activity 3: It's Not About You: Understanding the Influence of Personal Biases in Interpreting Messages

As you have read in this chapter and have learned in lecture and/or from your course textbook, various personal and contextual factors can have a great influence on your personal biases, and subsequently, these personal biases can influence your interpretation of received messages. This happens relatively frequently, and oftentimes we are not consciously aware of this powerful influence on our interpretation of received messages. A great way to objectively observe the influence of personal and contextual factors on one's personal biases and message interpretation is through television shows and film.

Watch one of your favourite television shows or films (sport-related, or not). As you are watching, take notes on various personal and contextual factors that influence various characters' personal biases (and consequently, message interpretations) during interpersonal communications. Select the three most (subjectively) interesting examples and summarize them, being sure to: (1) identify the *intended* message of the message sender; (2) explain the various personal and/or contextual factors influencing the message receiver's personal bias(es); (3) explain how these personal biases influenced the message receiver's interpretation of the received message(s); (4) discuss whether you think the presence of these personal biases helped or hurt the individual regarding their interpretation; and (5) explain why you found this example to be one of the most subjectively interesting examples from the show or film that you watched.

Putting It All Together

Creating a Personalized Effective Communication 'Crib Sheet'

This Putting It All Together activity is simple in concept but will require you to do quite a bit of critical thinking and self-reflection. Your Try It Out! activities will definitely help you here. Notice that this activity has relatively few rules regarding how your final product will visually look. This is because we want you to create something that is uniquely yours! This will maximize the likelihood that you will use this crib sheet, and that you will remember *how* to use it each time you review it.

Create a highly individualized crib sheet. This sheet is for *you*: this means that the specific guidelines, notes, or instructions that you put on it address *your* personal strengths and weaknesses in interpersonal communications. This should not be an exhaustive "all I ever wanted to know about effective communication" piece—it needs to be specifically designed for *you*. Frame all guidelines, notes, or instructions in positive terms (i.e., "do this" instead of "*don't* do this" terms).

Again, visually, this crib sheet can be anything you like. Your only guidelines for this crib sheet are: (1) It should make sense to you; (2) It must clearly identify message sending, message receiving, and message interpretation affect, behaviours, or cognitions you should perform during any interpersonal communication; and (3) It should be concise and user-friendly—think a single page, with minimal words. We recommend that you review this crib sheet before any important interpersonal communication you engage in, whether it is within your sport, or not.

Suggested Readings and References

Bandura, A. (1997). *Self-efficacy: The exercise of control*. New York: Freeman.

Billings, A. C., Butterworth, M. L., & Turman, P. D. (2012). *Communication and sport: Surveying the field*. Thousand Oaks, CA: Sage Publications.

Crocker, P. R. E. (2011). *Sport and exercise psychology: A Canadian perspective* (2nd ed.). Toronto: Pearson.

Eales-White, R. (1998). *Ask the right question!: How to get what you want every time and in every situation*. New York: McGraw-Hill.

Weinberg, R. S., & Gould, D. (2007). *Foundations of sport and exercise psychology* (4th ed.), Champaign, IL: Human Kinetics.

Williams. J. M. (2010). *Applied sport psychology: Personal growth to peak performance* (6th ed.). New York: McGraw-Hill.

Chapter 11

Peak Performance for Coaches

Key Concepts and Theories

- Psychological skills: competition planning, goal setting, imagery, self-talk, group dynamics, relaxation techniques, observational learning
- Leadership styles (e.g., autocratic, democratic)
- Burnout and stress

Using Mental Skills and Sharing Them with Others

Joe (reflecting to himself): "You know, I'm really having a good time coaching these pee-wee players. They have so much enthusiasm and love of hockey, it reminds me of what I was like at that age. I really want to help them keep this love of hockey and enjoy it throughout their lives. I know most of them will never get to enjoy the sport at the level I have, but it would be great if they could continue playing for life. Some might even become coaches when they get older. They would improve a lot, though, if they were able to concentrate more. They get so distracted! Sometimes I get distracted by the fans, the media, the pressure of the game, and being sore from the morning skate. I have some tricks I use to help me focus; maybe I can teach those to the kids too."

Psychological Skills for Coaches

Coaches frequently encourage their athletes to use psychological skills and acknowledge the importance of these skills for optimizing sport performance. In the vignette above Joe has learned to use psychological skills through his experiences as a professional hockey player and realizes those skills could be important for the youth team he is coaching. Coaches, however, may also benefit from using these skills in their coaching, and this concept is often neglected. Some recommendations for how coaches can use psychological skills are described below. Note that this list is not exhaustive and the reader is encouraged to think of additional psychological skills that would benefit coaches and how coaches could integrate the skills into their coaching.

Precompetition, competition plans, and routines can help coaches feel ready for competition. Planning is the best way to deal with unexpected scenarios, such as having a backup transportation plan when the team van will not start on the way to the competition, and a shortened warm-up routine ready for the athletes when the team arrives at the venue behind schedule. A competition plan will help the coach and athletes focus on their goals for the competition and execute a plan that is suitable given the opponents, environment, and situation. Perhaps most importantly, having routines leading up to competition can help coaches feel confident and in control. Familiarity brings comfort, and this is essential when under pressure to perform.

- **Goal setting**. Coaches benefit not only by setting goals for their athletes for competitions and training but also by setting personal coaching-related goals. For example, a coach may set a goal of providing more specific feedback to their players. This can be accomplished by tracking how many times they use generic feedback (e.g., "Good job!") versus specific feedback (e.g., "You followed through on your throw; that's great!").
- **Imagery**. Coaches can use imagery when planning game plans, routines, or race strategies. Coaches may image the opposition, competition environment, the athletes they coach, potential situations in the competition, and possible responses by their athletes. In training environments coaches can use imagery of specific sport skills to compare the technique of the athletes they coach to an ideal model.
- **Self-talk**. Coaches can use self-talk for reasons similar to athletes, that is, assist with teaching and refining sport skills, develop or modify strategies, formulate goals, psych up or relax, and feel confident and focused. For example, a coach who wants to control his emotions and have confidence in his players might make the self-talk statement: "Take a deep breath; they did this play in practice the other day and it went fine; they'll remember it."
- **Group processes**. There are many group processes that can help or hinder coaching success. Often the coach is the person most responsible for the group dynamics within their team. A coach, however, is also influenced by these dynamics. For example, a coach must understand and accept their role on the team. This can be difficult for some coaches when there is demand on them to fulfill several roles that may conflict with each other. Consider the coach of a youth hockey team in a small town who is also the mother of one of the players and the school physical education teacher. This coach must find a balance between her roles as coach, mother, and teacher, and balance the conflicts that may be created because of the demands of these different roles.
- **Focus**. Just as with athletes, it is important for coaches to be able to shift their attention to appropriate cues. For example, a volleyball coach must be able to observe his own team as well as the opposition. The volleyball coach notes the quality of the pass from his player, the selection of the setter for which hitter to set, the shot selection of the hitter, whether there was a block set by the defense, and which shots were successful against the defense.
- **Anxiety**. Relaxation techniques such as deep-centered breathing can help coaches get their physical symptoms (e.g., increased rate of respiration) under control and focus on the critical moments in the game when their decisions may influence the outcome.
- **Modeling**. Less-experienced coaches are frequently matched with mentor coaches who assist the development of coaching behaviours. A developing coach learns effective instruction techniques by observing a mentor coach teach a technical sport skill to an athlete by breaking the skill into manageable parts and explaining the cause and effect of performing the skill in that manner. The developing coach would then see the athlete have an effective outcome (i.e., perform the skill correctly) and

decide to incorporate into their coaching the instruction technique of skill breakdown paired with providing a rationale.

Coaches' Encouragement of Athletes' Use of Psychological Skills

Coaches who participated in sport at a relatively high level and have taken coach education courses tend to reinforce the use of mental skills by their athletes. Coaches are influential in athletes' use of mental skills as they are best situated to incorporate psychological skills into practice settings, reinforce their importance, and introduce the skills to make the athlete aware of them and their benefits. It is important to remember though that coaches should use and encourage the use of psychological skills on a regular basis, but the coach should not take on the role of sport psychologist. Many coaches acknowledge the importance of psychological skills but fail to make them a priority. An approach of introducing a sport psychology concept at the beginning of a training session and then giving athletes an opportunity to try the skill during training is a resource-efficient method of encouraging the use of psychological skills. Once the athletes have some practice with the psychological skill they can incorporate it into competition settings, just as they would gradually introduce new physical skills and game plays into competition. An example of this process is given in the vignette below. Try it yourself in the Try It Out! Activity 1, on page 174.

Incorporating Sport Psychology

Joe as coach: "Hi everyone. In practice today we're going to work on focusing. When we're focused we are paying attention only to what is important to hockey. What kinds of things do you think are important to pay attention to in hockey?"

Athletes: "Who has the puck. The referee. The time in the game. Where your teammates are."

C: "Good answers. What kinds of things are not important and can distract you from playing your best?"

A: "When it's cold in the rink. Parents yelling. When I make a mistake."

C: "Great job. Those things can definitely be distracting. Sometimes we get distracted in practice, too, like when your friend wants to tell you a story or you're getting tired near the end of practice. Sometimes you need to ask your friends to tell you their story after practice so you can concentrate on what you're working on. Or, when you're tired, you might need to remind yourself of what you want to focus on like following through on your shot. Everyone pick up a puck. Now let's see if you can concentrate only on the puck for thirty seconds. Ready? Go. Good work. You can work on this at home, too. Today during training I want you to try to pay attention to when you are not focused. Think about what things make it hard for you to concentrate. See if you can bring your focus back to what you're supposed to be doing. Okay, let's go finish our warm-up."

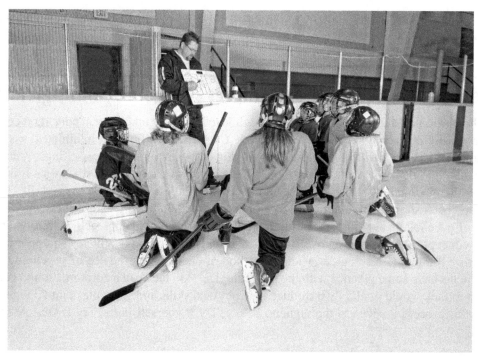

© Lorraine Swanson, 2012. Used under license from Shutterstock, Inc.

Coaching Behaviours

Observe and interview a coach in a sport of your choice. Your observations may include the following:

- Note how the coach teaches skills and strategies.
- What does the coach communicate to the athletes following competitive success? Failure?
- How does the coach react to player feedback and comments?
- What techniques does the coach use to motivate the athletes?
- What methods does the coach use to recognize and reward strong performance?
- What kind of relationships does the coach have with the athletes?
- What does the team atmosphere feel like?

> ### Deep Thoughts
>
> Recall some coaches you have had. Think about how they have influenced you in sport and in life. What positive influences have they had? Did they have any negative influences? What could the coach have done differently? How would this have affected you and/or the team?

Observe whether what the coach says in the interview is reflected in her or his behaviour with the athletes. Some interview questions that may be useful to ask include the following:

- Does the coach have final authority in decisions or do they make joint decisions with the athletes/ team captains/coaching staff?
- How does the coach articulate a vision for the team/athletes?
- How does the coach convince the athletes to buy into the vision?
- Does the coach initiate discussions about leadership with the athletes? If so, what is included in these discussions?

In your observation and interview, consider what behaviours are required of the coach in their coaching context (e.g., organizing transportation to tournaments, discussing fair play with parents). Consider what the preferred coach behaviours of the athletes may be, this may be influenced by the athletes' demographic characteristics including, for example: age, gender, sport, and competition level.

Several tools have been developed to assess coach behaviour. Many of these measures assess the coach in terms of their leadership behaviours. One common inventory of coach leadership behaviours is the Coaching Behavioral Assessment System (CBAS; Smith, Smoll, & Hunt, 1977). The twelve categories of leader behaviours are observed and recorded. These behaviours include both reactive behaviours (e.g., praising a player for a good play) and spontaneous behaviours that a coach initiates (e.g., assigning player positions prior to the start of the game). Complete the Try It Out! Activity 2 near the end of this chapter. Exercises such as this are useful for coaches to affirm that their coaching behaviours are congruent with their objectives and coaching philosophy.

Burnout

Burnout and stress of the coach not only affects them, but their athletes as well. Symptoms of burnout in coaches are similar to symptoms of depression and may include indicators such as mood swings, negative affect (emotions), heightened anxiety, mental and physical exhaustion, difficulty sleeping, problems concentrating, and lack of energy.

Burnout can be addressed or prevented by having a social support system in place. This support system may be a significant other (e.g., wife, husband, close friend) who is supportive regardless of the success or failures of the coach; a mentor or coaching colleague who is able to empathise with the coach and provide advice; the coaching or administrative staff in the coaching environment who has shared experiences and can remind the coach to maintain perspective.

Another strategy for preventing burnout is to use the psychological skills described earlier in this chapter and throughout the book. Positive self-talk, for example, can help coaches maintain a positive view of their coaching success and put criticism from the media, fans, and parents in context. Relaxation techniques to cope with anxiety is a technique commonly taught to athletes, coaches may experience even more anxiety than their athletes—some examples: success or failure may determine the coach's employment status and income; once the competition begins the coach has limited control over what the athletes do. Taking time for vacations with family and friends will further strengthen their social support

© aceshot1, 2012. Used under license from Shutterstock, Inc.

network and allow opportunities to mentally take a break from coaching. Finally, coaches spend a lot of their time ensuring the athletes they coach are in optimal physical condition. In turn, however, they often sacrifice their own physical condition. Coaches who are in better physical condition will find it easier to cope with the physical and mental demands of their career. Specifically, it is easier to demonstrate sport specific skills when a coach has a sound level of physical fitness. A healthy body is also more resistant to psychological stressors.

Summary: Putting It All Together

Many coaches acknowledge the importance of psychological skills but struggle with how or when to use them in training and competition. With creativity these skills can be incorporated into the practice drills and activities that coaches already use. By reflecting on how, when, and why they use these psychological skills themselves coaches may realize the athletes they coach would receive similar benefits from the skills. Using psychological skills can also help coaches be more effective and avoid burnout. Complete the Putting It All Together activity in this chapter to gain a better understanding of factors related to coach burnout.

Try It Out!

Activity 1: Incorporating Psychological Skills

Select a sport you have experience with and a psychological skill you have a clear understanding of. Specific to your selected sport detail how you would introduce the psychological skill into the practice setting and how you would progress the skill throughout the season and into competition environments.

Activity 2: Observing Coach Behaviours

If you are a coach have someone else assess your coaching behaviour using a tool such as the CBAS. Be sure to get the results following the assessment. Alternatively, ask a coach you know if you may assess his or her coaching behaviour. Be sure you understand the assessment tool you are using and give the coach constructive feedback following the assessment.

Putting It All Together

Look through newspapers and popular magazines (online or print) and find a story about coach burnout from the past five years. Find out more about the coach and his or her coaching environment. What factors can you identify that may have contributed to burnout? Now, imagine that you could go back in time and help the coach prevent burnout when the symptoms first started to appear. Detail a plan of what the prevention program would look like and provide a rationale for why this plan would help.

Suggested Readings and References

Andrew, D. P. S., & Kent, A. (2007). The impact of perceived leadership behaviours on satisfaction, commitment, and motivation: An expansion of the multidimensional model of leadership. *International Journal of Coaching Science, 1* (1), 37–58.

Crocker, P. R. E. (2011). *Sport and exercise psychology: A Canadian perspective*, 2nd ed. Toronto, Ontario: Pearson Canada.

Smith, R. E., Smoll, F. L., & Hunt, E. (1977). A system for the behavioral assessment of athletic coaches. *Research Quarterly, 48*, 401–407.

Tenenbaum, G., & Eklund, R. (2007). *Handbook of sport psychology*, 3rd ed. Hoboken, NJ: Wiley.

Weinberg, R. S., & Gould, D. (2003). *Foundations of sport and exercise psychology*, 3rd ed. Champaign, IL: Human Kinetics.

Chapter 12

Psychology of Physical Activity

Key Concepts and Theories

- Behaviour change theories covered in your class (e.g., health protection model, self-determination theory, stages of change, theory of planned behaviour)
- Psychological skills (e.g., imagery, self-talk, attention control, goal setting)
- Environmental approaches to behaviour change
- Information delivery approaches to behaviour change
- Social approaches to behaviour change (e.g., team building, social support)

Making a Change

Eric is 36 years old, works at a desk job for the federal government, is married to Melissa, and has two young children. Recently Eric has noticed he lacks energy to play with his kids. He used to play sports in high school but since then has not been very active. He's also concerned about his health; last year his dad was diagnosed with Type II diabetes. Eric is exploring options to be more active for both health and social benefits. Activities he has considered joining are recreational co-ed volleyball (he and Melissa could play together), a neighbourhood early morning bootcamp, and the badminton program at the nearby racquet club. However, Eric knows that changing his lifestyle might be a challenge at times, so he wants to find activities where he can rely on friends, family, or people he meets as a support network.

Sport Psychology Skills as "Exercise Psychology Skills"?

As you have read through this book, you may have noticed that much of our discussion of the topics was in relation to sport participation, whether at the recreational level or at the competitive level. However, many of the psychological skills and concepts discussed in these chapters also apply to exercise settings. In fact, research examining psychological skills (e.g., imagery, self-talk, and goal setting) among exercisers finds that regular exercisers use these skills more frequently than insufficiently active and sedentary individuals. Individuals who use these skills also report more confidence or self-efficacy for exercise. Individuals can also use some of these skills to help manage anxiety experienced in the exercise setting. For example, individuals with a high level of social physique anxiety (SPA) feel anxious about their bodies being judged by others. You can imagine how certain exercise settings may increase or decrease feelings of SPA. In this chapter we will explore how these skills, and other techniques, can be used to encourage individuals to start and stick with a regular exercise program.

Deep Thought

Do you ever have trouble fitting exercise or healthy eating into your day? What are your biggest challenges to eating healthy and being active? How do you manage these challenges? Discuss your thoughts with a partner.

If PA Is So Good for Us, Why Aren't More People Physically Active?

As a student in a physical education, kinesiology, coaching, or recreation and leisure studies program, you likely have a positive view of the benefits of physical activity. You may also be committed to incorporating physical activity into your daily routine. However, research tells us that this is not the norm for many people. Numerous reports show that the majority of children, adolescents, and adults in North America are insufficiently active—meaning they do not get enough physical activity to meet ACSM, WHO, or CSEP guidelines for physical activity and to achieve the health benefits of being physically active. Based on self-reported physical activity, approximately 49 percent of American (Carlson et al., 2011) and 52 percent of Canadian adults are physically active (Statistics Canada, 2010). However, more objective accelerometer data tells us the number of adults who are actually meeting physical activity guidelines is much lower—with only 15 percent of Canadian adults meeting current physical activity guidelines (Colley et al., 2011a). The story is similar with respect to children and youth. In Canada, accelerometer data shows that only 7 percent of children and youth meet current physical activity guidelines (Colley et al., 2011b). The question is: Why?

Over the years, various theories have been used to try and explain people's physical activity behaviour. Some theories have been borrowed from other areas of psychology (e.g., self-determination theory, self-efficacy theory), while others have been developed specifically with exercise and other health behaviours in mind (e.g., health protection model). Regardless of which theory you prefer, all of these theories add some insight into the reasons why people engage in or avoid physical activity. The theories used to explain physical activity behaviour can also be grouped according to commonalities—shared or similar concepts that are included in several theories.

The major theories and models used to explain physical activity behaviour and that are included in most textbooks on exercise psychology include: theory of reasoned action, theory of planned behaviour, the transtheoretical model (stages of change), social cognitive theory (including self-efficacy theory), health belief model, protection motivation theory, self-determination theory, and social ecological models. In your course readings, you may have covered some or all of these theories. Consider how these theories can be grouped together in terms of what they have in common, and how they may differ. Which theories consider the exerciser's thoughts and beliefs toward exercise (e.g., attitudes)? Which examine their feelings and self-perceptions (e.g., confidence, self-efficacy, motivation)? Which consider the environment (e.g., social support, norms for physical activity, physical environment)? Do several different theories contain concepts that are quite similar? For example, confidence and self-efficacy both reflect an individual's belief in his or her own abilities; however, confidence is a more global construct while self-efficacy is task specific. Complete Try It Out! Activity 1 on page 191 to help you explore how your own physical activity behaviour can be explained by one of the exercise psychology theories.

Strategies to Promote Physical Activity Adherence

Once you have an understanding of *why* people may or may not engage in physical activity, your next question is likely: *how can we get someone to start being more active?* Within your sport and exercise psychology course, you may have discussed different strategies for motivating people to become active. These strategies can be organized according to the approach they take. For example, some are theory-based, while others are behavioural or environmental approaches. Other strategies focus on the delivery method: how is the information and physical activity message communicated to the population? In this section we will explore each of these approaches.

Theory-based Strategies

Now that you've examined different theories and evaluated how well they explain your physical activity behaviour, we will consider how you might use those theories to create an intervention that helps to change people's physical activity behaviour. Let's take the example of the theory of planned behaviour. Considerable research shows that the constructs of subjective norm, attitudes, and perceived behavioural control all influence an individual's intention to engage in physical activity. However, one of the main challenges is translating this increased intention into actual behaviour. How many times have you, or someone you know, said "Yeah, sign me up for that," only to cancel or change your plans? Faced with this problem, researchers have tried to devise interventions that target concepts within the theory (e.g., increasing the strength of intentions) in order to have a more powerful effect on behaviour. One such example is the use of implementation intentions. These are specific plans that ask individuals to identify not only *what* they intend to do (e.g., go to the gym), but *when* (e.g., before work) and *how* they are going to carry out the intended action (e.g., run on the treadmill for 30 minutes). Essentially people are asked to create a plan for translating their intentions into behaviour.

Now that you've seen how theory-based interventions work, select one of the theories you studied in class. Based on the research discussed in class, what aspect of the theory would you target in order to have the largest impact on someone's likelihood of being active? Complete Try It Out! Activity 2 on page 193.

Behavioural Approaches

Another approach to changing physical activity behaviour is to target *what* the individual does directly, that is, his or her behaviour. These interventions can be based on theory, but they may also focus on specific behavioural strategies that have been shown to work. Reflect back on the previous chapters in this book using the list of sport psychology strategies below. How might you apply each to a physical activity setting?

- Goal setting
- Imagery
- Self-talk
- Arousal regulation
- Attention control
- Team building

Let's take self-talk as an example. Research examining how exercisers use self-talk has shown that they use it for specific functions, or reasons: to improve or learn new exercise technique, to motivate themselves, to control energy levels, and to feel confident in their abilities. Studies examining self-talk among different groups of exercisers and non-exercisers show that people who use self-talk more frequently in relation to exercise also tend to be more frequent exercisers. Therefore, an intervention that has new exercisers use specific self-talk statements related to exercise thoughts, feelings, and behaviours may help to increase the amount of time that those new exercisers are physically active. Complete Try It Out! Activity 3 on page 195 to develop self-talk statements for Eric. Once you have completed Activity 3, move on to Activity 4 on page 197 to help you apply other psychological skills as part of an exercise intervention.

Environmental Approaches

The environment in which we do physical activity can also play a huge role in our experience and willingness to participate. Consider your school's athletic facility: what characteristics of the physical space make it inviting? What characteristics might make it uninviting for certain individuals? Now, think about the social environment, that is, the people in the facility, the staff, the "feeling" of the social climate in the gym, how people interact, the values or mission statement of the facility, and how it is conveyed to the members. Do those factors make it inviting or uninviting? These aspects of the physical and social environment are factors that researchers may target within a physical activity intervention.

Deep Thought

Think about the different places where you, and others, are physically active (e.g., parks, sport and/or fitness facilities, school playgrounds, beaches). Using magazines, the internet, or your own photos, find a variety of images representing different physical activity environments. Which represent inviting versus uninviting physical activity environments? What elements make an environment more or less appealing?

Select a physical activity space in your community. Visit that place and identify the aspects that encourage versus discourage activity. What could the community do to make it more inviting? Tip: Consider community programs (e.g., bike rentals), environmental features (e.g., sidewalks, bike paths, grassy spaces), and individual factors. For example, the elements that make a space physical activity–friendly may differ for children, teens, older adults, and individuals with limited mobility.

Deep Thought

Think about the last time you went to a group fitness class. Did you enjoy it? Why or why not? Think about how you felt about the instructor and how he/she ran the class. Were the other class members friendly and welcoming? Did you feel out of place or part of a group?

Research provides strong support for the idea that having a social support system—friends, family, significant others, pets, health care providers—that supports our physical activity behaviour and encourages it is important for helping us to get active and stick with it. Interventions that help to provide exercisers with social support can also be an important part of changing physical activity behaviour.

Think about the theories you've discussed in your course that relate to social support. Perhaps you discussed how self-efficacy can be increased through seeing others be successful (e.g., exercise role models), or how a sense of belonging (i.e., relatedness) is important for self-determined behaviour.

The study of group dynamics, covered in Chapter 9 in this book, also gives us some insight into how we can change the social environment to encourage physical activity. While the coach or team captain provides important leadership to a sport team, the fitness class instructor serves as a leader for exercisers. To help you explore how team building can be applied to an exercise setting, consider the following example:

Eric decides that he will try the bootcamp class run by the local fitness club. On the first day of class he is quite nervous. He has never done this sort of training and is worried about looking stupid because he isn't familiar with the exercises and thinks the other class members all look much fitter than him. He's not sure how the instructor will run the class: Will he yell at them and single people out? Eric gets to the class a few minutes early. The instructor greets him at the door and introduces himself. He starts the class by saying, "This is an introductory class for people who have never tried bootcamp before. We're going to start off with the basics so you all learn how to do the exercises correctly. By the end of the 8 weeks, you'll be pros at this. Be sure to work at your own pace as we go along!"

Using the components of the team building model as a guide, what are some factors that might influence how much Eric feels as though he fits into this group? What could the instructor do to help build a sense of cohesion within the class (e.g., consider leadership style, communication, group norms, etc.)?

Delivery Methods

To encourage people to be active, health promoters and researchers must also consider *how* they get the message out to the public. In order for people to join a new gym, they have to know it's there and what programs are offered. The delivery method is a key consideration when designing physical activity interventions. Delivery methods may include the form of communication used (e.g., television, radio, telephone, online, word of mouth) as well as how the message is communicated (e.g., gain framed vs. loss framed).

Deep Thought

Each method for delivering a message has its pros and cons. With a partner, make a list of the pros and cons for each of the following informational approaches: mass media campaigns, community-wide campaigns, point of decision prompts. Which do you think would be most effective for changing behaviour on an **individual level**? What about at the **population** level? Debate your choices with your partner.

Now that we've examined the pros and cons of each approach, let's take a look at an actual campaign and see whether its design matches up with what you've learned in class about targeting physical activity messages. Complete Try It Out! Activity 5 on page 199 to evaluate an existing physical activity promotion campaign.

Summary: Putting It All Together

In this chapter we've explored how various factors can influence an individual's physical activity behaviour. Indeed, it is clear that there is no single or perfect solution for changing behaviour; however, small changes in various aspects related to the individual, the message, and the environment may combine to impact someone's behaviour. Eric's struggle to increase his physical activity level is one that is shared by many people in today's society. Consider how you can apply what you have learned about behaviour change to your own life. As a challenge, use the Putting It All Together activity in this chapter to try and create a plan for changing your own worst health habit; perhaps it will be to increase your physical activity level, eat more fruits and vegetables, drink more water, or reduce your alcohol or junk food consumption.

Try It Out!

Activity 1: Theories of Physical Activity

Select one theory used in your course that explains PA behaviour.

A. Draw a diagram showing the relationship between concepts in that theory.

B. For each concept, indicate how it relates to your life and your own barriers to physical activity (e.g., for the Theory of Planned Behaviour, to what extent do you feel as though you're in control of when, where, and how you are physically active?). You may want to go back to your diagram and add key words that reflect your own example to link specific aspects of your example to specific concepts in the theory. Having an example from your own life, or from those around you, will help you to better remember the individual theories and see how they are similar and different.

C. Once you have completed the activity with your chosen theory, complete the activity again using another theory.

D. Are there theories that offer a better explanation of your thoughts, feelings, and behaviour than others?

Activity 2: Designing Theory-Based Interventions

Design an intervention strategy that targets one aspect of your chosen theory from Activity 1. Make sure you address each of the following questions.

A. Which element of the theory will you target? Depending on the theory, consider whether targeting one aspect of the model is key or if you need to target multiple aspects at once. Keep in mind that often the simplest strategies are the most effective; they are easy for people to understand and follow through with.

B. What will you ask people to do?

C. How will they complete it (e.g., paper and pencil, discussion, etc.)?

D. How will you evaluate whether your intervention was successful? Your evaluation should be related to the theoretical construct you targeted as well as your desired outcome.

Activity 3: Developing Self-Talk Statements

Using the table below, try to come up with an example of a self-talk statement that would help Eric in each of the situations below.

Situation	Function	Self-Talk Statement
It's Eric's first class of bootcamp. He is trying to remember correct squatting technique.	Skill function	
Near the end of the workout, Eric is feeling tired but knows he only has three more reps to do.	Increase arousal	
This week has been crazy. Eric's children all have the flu and his wife is out of town. He is having trouble motivating himself to go to the gym.	Increase drive	
Eric and his wife have entered the recreational-level badminton tournament at their local racquet club. He is feeling a bit rusty and wants to feel confident before their first game.	Mastery	

Activity 4: Sport Psychology Skills Are Exercise Psychology Skills, Too!

Select one of the sport psychology skills listed in the chapter (e.g., goal setting, imagery, self-talk, modeling, arousal regulation, attention control) or that you have covered in your class. Describe how you would apply that skill to the following exercisers (e.g., when, where, why, and how):

A. A new exerciser who is trying to begin and stick with an exercise program—Eric, for example.
B. Someone who started an exercise program within the last 6 months and is trying to stick with it.
C. Someone who has been exercising regularly for the last few years but wants to continue increasing the challenge and building his or her fitness level.

Activity 5: Evaluating a Physical Activity Promotion Campaign

Select an existing physical activity promotion campaign. Find promotional materials (e.g., website, pamphlet, commercial, posters, etc.) advertising the campaign. You can select a campaign advertised at your local health center, a national campaign, or a school-based initiative. Based on what you know about physical activity behaviour, analyze the content of the campaign according to the elements listed below.

    A. Who is the target audience?
    B. Is it theory based? If so, identify the theory.
    C. What physical activity-related psychological constructs does it target?
    D. What type(s) of strategies does it use to promote physical activity?
    E. Do you think it is effective? Why or why not?

Bonus Question: Put yourself in the position of the program administrator. If you were responsible for running this campaign and/or administering this program, how would you figure out if it is achieving its goals? Explain how you would test whether or not the campaign is effective.

Putting It All Together

Pick one intervention strategy we have discussed in this book (or chapter). Plan how you will use it to change one health behaviour. Track your progress over 2 to 4 weeks. How successful were you? What challenges did you face? Fill in the chart below to plan and describe your experience.

My Target Health Behaviour	
Intervention Strategy	
Description of Intervention	
Method for Tracking Progress	
Challenges faced During the Intervention	
Method of Evaluating Success	
Success of Intervention	
Changes for Next Time	

Implementation Intention Worksheet

Target Behaviour:
When and Where?
How will you accomplish this? (details):
Translate this into a specific statement. For example:

Each lunch hour, when I go to the cafeteria for lunch (when/where), I will buy an apple for a snack rather than a bag of chips (target behaviour).

Create your specific implementation intention:

Suggested Readings and References

Carlson, S. A., Fulton, J. E., Galuska, D. A., & Kruger, J. (2005). Prevalence of self-reported physically active adults—United States, 2007. *MMWR Weekly, 57*(48), 1297–1300.

Colley, R. C., Garriguet, D., Janssen, I., Craig, C. L., Clarke, J., & Tremblay, M. S. (2011a). Physical activity of Canadian adults: Accelerometer results from the 2007 to 2009 Canadian Health Measures Survey. *Health Reports, 22*(1), 7–14. Statistics Canada, Catalogue no. 82-003-XPE.

Colley, R. C., Garriguet, D., Janssen, I., Craig, C. L., Clarke, J., & Tremblay, M. S. (2011b). Physical activity of Canadian children and youth: Accelerometer results from the 2007 to 2009 Canadian Health Measures Survey. *Health Reports, 22*(1), 15–23. Statistics Canada, Catalogue no. 82-003-XPE.

Crocker, P. R. E. (2011). *Sport and exercise psychology: A Canadian perspective* (2nd ed.). Toronto: Pearson.

Heath, G. W., Brownson, R. C., Kruger, J., Miles, R., Powell, K. E., Ramsey, L. T., and the Task Force on Community Preventive Services. (2006). The effectiveness of urban design and land use and transportation policies and practices to increase physical activity: A systematic review. *Journal of Physical Activity and Health, 3*(1S), S55–S76.

Kahn, E. B., Ramsey, L. T., Brownson, R. C., Heath, G. W., Howe, E. H., Powell, K. E., et al. (2002). The effectiveness of interventions to increase physical activity: A systematic review. *American Journal of Preventive Medicine, 22*(4S), 73–107.

Latimer, A. E., Rench, T. A., Rivers, S. E., Katulak, N. A., Materese, S. A., Cadmus, L., et al. (2008). Promoting participation in physical activity using framed messages: An application of prospect theory. *British Journal of Health Psychology, 13,* 659–681.

Lox, C. L., Martin Ginis, K. A., & Petruzzello, S. J. (2010). *The psychology of exercise: Integrating theory and practice* (3rd ed.). Scottsdale, AZ: Holcolm Hathaway.

Statistics Canada. (2010). *Physical activity during leisure time, 2009* (Catalogue 82–625). Ottawa, ON: Statistics Canada. Available at: http://statcan.gc.ca/pub/82-625-x/2010002/article/11267-eng.htm.

Weinberg, R. S., & Gould, D. (2007). *Foundations of sport and exercise psychology* (4th ed.), Champaign, IL: Human Kinetics.

CPSIA information can be obtained
at www.ICGtesting.com
Printed in the USA
LVHW021518111219
639988LV00002B/2/P

9 781465 207463